# RAIF BADAWI,
# THE VOICE OF FREEDOM

# RAIF BADAWI,
# THE VOICE OF FREEDOM

## MY HUSBAND, OUR STORY

## Ensaf Haidar
## & Andrea C. Hoffmann

Translated from the German
by Shaun Whiteside

OTHER PRESS
NEW YORK

Production editor: Yvonne E. Cárdenas

Typeset in Minion by M Rules

1 3 5 7 9 10 8 6 4 2

Library of Congress Cataloging-in-Publication Data

Names: Haidar, Ensaf, author. | Hoffmann, Andrea Claudia, author. |
Whiteside, Shaun, translator.
Title: Raif Badawi, the voice of freedom : my husband, our story /
Ensaf Haidar and Andrea Claudia Hoffmann ; translated by Shaun Whiteside.
Other titles: Freiheit für Raif Badawi, die Liebe meines Lebens.
English Description: New York : Other Press, 2016.
Identifiers: LCCN 2016000397 | ISBN 9781590518014 (hardback) |
ISBN 9781590518021 (ebook)
Subjects: LCSH: Badawi, Raif, 1984– | Political prisoners—Saudi Arabia. |
Dissidents—Saudi Arabia. | BISAC: BIOGRAPHY & AUTOBIOGRAPHY /
Political. | BIOGRAPHY & AUTOBIOGRAPHY / Personal Memoirs.
Classification: LCC DS244.526.B33 H35 2016 | DDC 365/.45092—dc23
LC record available at http://lccn.loc.gov/2016000397

# RAIF BADAWI,
# THE VOICE OF FREEDOM

# INTRODUCTION

The weather is bad as we stand outside Sherbrooke town hall. The rain is pouring down — as it does so often in my new home, Canada, which is in every respect the opposite of my old one.

All my friends have come. It has been almost four years since my husband Raif Badawi was arrested in Jeddah, Saudi Arabia. Since then he has been in jail. One year ago, he was publicly whipped in front of a big mosque in the city.

"Freedom for Raif," my friend Jane shouts into her megaphone. The other people taking part in the demonstration repeat her call. They are a few dozen loyal companions who gather with me here, week after week. We hold up orange posters with huge black letters to make Raif's name. We express our demand: *"Libérez Raif* — free Raif!"

Later, when we sit together in a Lebanese restaurant near the town hall, warming ourselves up, Jeff comes over to me. He's the guitarist with the Canadian band Your Favorite Enemies. Today he's joined us to support us in our struggle.

He solemnly hands me a bundle of letters. "This is mail

from our fans, Mrs. Haidar," he tells me. "They want to give you and Raif the courage to keep going."

"*Merci* — thanks," I say to him and, touched, take the bundle from him. "Your solidarity is very important for us."

By now, luckily, I can speak enough French to express myself in the language. That hasn't been the case for long: when we arrived in Quebec in autumn 2013 I had to sit behind a school desk like a little girl and learn how to communicate. My children Najwa, Dodi and Miriam could speak at least a little French after our previous stay in Lebanon. I spoke only Arabic.

It wasn't the only change that I found difficult. Since I was forced to flee from Saudi Arabia, pretty much everything in my life has changed. For the first time I had to learn how to take responsibility for myself and my family as a woman on her own. North American culture was completely alien to me. The food smelled and tasted different, the cold climate put a terrible strain on me and I didn't know anyone in this country, whose social rules were so unfamiliar to me.

I don't mean that the people I met in Canada were in any way unpleasant or unfriendly. On the contrary: they welcomed me with open arms, and from the very first I liked their casual, open manners. But it was alien to me nonetheless.

I have experienced boundless support in the country that granted us asylum. Asylum from the state where I was brought up and formed, where many of the people I love still live. Asylum from the country that threatens my husband with death. And I can't say how grateful I am for that: side by side with people from all over the world, I can devote myself effectively here to the liberation of my husband.

Najwa, Dodi and Miriam acclimatized much more

quickly than I did, as children do. As for me, shortly after we arrived abroad I threatened to slip into depression in the face of the cruelty and hopelessness of Raif's situation.

But while I was in danger of giving up, I began to understand what a waste that would be. A waste of freedom, strength and opportunities to develop. A waste of everything that Raif has stood for. A waste of the love that I am allowed to experience with him.

My name, Ensaf, has a wide range of meanings in Arabic, from "justice" to "patience." In my current struggle on Raif's behalf I often have the feeling that I urgently need all of these different facets. It's all in a name, as they say.

Once — compared to now — I was spoiled. I had nothing to worry about, but I had no responsibilities either. Today a great weight rests on my shoulders. But my task has made me grow as a person. And I have noticed how strong I can be when I want to achieve something. I can express my thoughts and speak in public. Back when I lived with my parents and was sheltered from everything and everyone in the world I would never have thought any of that possible.

To that extent I have personally profited from my commitment to freeing Raif: he has made me strong. Stronger than I could ever have dreamed as a traditionally brought up Saudi woman. That's a good experience.

I thank Jeff for the letters and try on the silk scarf that he hands me as a gift. In my former life I might have worn it as a headscarf; today I prefer to wear it around my neck. "I'm very grateful to you for your support of Raif and freedom of expression," I assure him.

"But it's our duty, Mrs. Haidar," he says with a smile, "And please say hi to Raif from us next time you talk to him."

I don't know how our fight will go. Spellbound, I watch the news from home, the effect of which is like an emotional roller coaster. Sometimes it gives me hope, then I despair again. Will I, and our many supporters all over the world, manage to save my beloved husband? Or will my children and I have to watch the police in Jeddah beating him to death one day?

Only one thing is certain: my children and I will fight for him to our last breath.

# CHAPTER ONE

# A FORBIDDEN LOVE

My first mobile phone was a silver-colored model with rubber keys. When my sister Hanan pressed the phone into my hand, neither of us knew that it would open the gates of the world to me.

Hanan had been given the phone as a wedding present, and didn't really know what to do with it. She thought the landline should be enough for a married woman. But I, a student of Qur'anic studies, could for example call home if the driver who collected me from the university every day didn't turn up on time.

So for the first time I now had an autonomous connection with the world outside of my parents' house. In my home country, Saudi Arabia, where young women are guarded like crown jewels until their wedding, that was extremely unusual. Too much freedom is seen as a risk. And in fact from now on risk would become a fixed quantity in my life, which had been so placid until then.

I had been a student of Qur'anic studies for the previous two years, although without any great ambitions. Getting a job after university was not part of my life plan. My father is affluent, and a career for his daughters or wives is out of the question as far as he's concerned. We just don't need it. He is one of the local dignitaries of my home town of Jizan, and makes so much money from his furniture business that he has no trouble keeping a large house and two families: he has eleven children with my mother and another four with a younger woman. It's not proper for his daughters or wives to work outside of the house.

But since I now had a mobile phone, my sister Egbal advised me to register with the employment authorities. "At least try to get a job. If you give them your mobile number, Ensaf, no one at home will know if they actually call you. And in any case there's so much unemployment you'll wait years for an offer from them." Egbal is twelve years older than me — and already a widow, which forces her to live at home with us again, under my father's custodianship. No wonder that she nudged me cautiously in the direction of financial independence.

The only job that my father might have allowed me and Egbal was as a teacher in a Qur'an school. According to Islamic values the education of girls is an idle task, and in my family teaching is more or less the only acceptable job for a woman. That was fine: after going to such a school myself — and studying Qur'anic studies — I wasn't suited for another job in any case. So I registered as a teacher of religion looking for work. But I didn't really expect that filling in the forms would have any consequences. And in fact I didn't want it to: I had no professional ambitions or dreams. Living from day to day in my parents' house was quite enough for me.

When Egbal and I came home from our trip to the authorities in the afternoon, I threw my abaya, the shapeless black garment that we have to wear outside the house, in a corner, and took off my full-face veil, the niqab. Under that black uniform I wore a flowery summer dress, better suited to the temperatures in Saudi Arabia. I took a Coca-Cola from the fridge and withdrew to my room. There was a Turkish soap on television, and I eventually dozed off in front of its family dramas. When I woke up again I saw that I had missed a call.

It could only have been the employment agency. The woman from the office had said she would call if a job came up. But things were going far too quickly for me. In fact I had already prepared for several years' holiday: watching television until the small hours, sleeping late in the morning... Enjoying my time until my family married me off and I had to fulfill the duties of a wife.

So I waited until the end of the day before calling back, and just planned to leave a message on voice mail. At twenty past five I dialed call-back.

"Hello?" said a male voice.

"Oh, erm, hello," I stammered. "Your number showed on the display. Did you call me?"

"No," said the young man at the other end of the line. "Not that I'm aware of..."

"OK. Well in that case I'm sorry. Goodbye."

I hastily hung up. I was consumed with shame. I had phoned a male stranger! Just like that. What in heaven's name would he think of me?

While I reproached myself, the phone rang again. I stared at the display—and my heart skipped a beat. The same number.

Had he not just said he hadn't dialed my number? So why was he doing it now? I automatically took the call.

"Hello," he said again. His voice sounded nice, soft and full.

"Hello," I replied coolly.

"You have a beautiful voice," he said shyly. "Might you be interested in talking to me on the phone for a while?"

"Of course not!" I said furiously. My worries had been justified. He already saw me as a frivolous woman, I was sure of it. "I said I called by accident. I apologize."

"Oh, come on. Just for a few minutes," he asked.

"No, definitely not!"

I resolutely ended the call. The phone rang again. I hastily silenced the ringtone, so that my family wouldn't be aware of what was going on. My brothers would have been far from happy if they had known that a stranger was pestering me. To be quite safe from them, I cautiously locked my door.

Now my phone started flashing: I watched with fascination as the display lit up with every suppressed ring. Like a torch sending Morse signals: "SOS. PLEASE PICK UP!"

I spent the whole evening watching the light messages on my phone. The man — whoever he was — rang me twenty-five times in all. He refused to give up. And of course I was impressed by that.

In Saudi Arabia we normally have no opportunity to come into contact with the opposite sex. From puberty we girls can only leave the parental home veiled from head to foot. And we must never travel on our own. Schools — and all other areas of daily life — are strictly segregated by gender to prevent the possibility of unmarried women having chance encounters. So in my parents' house, for example, there are two sitting rooms: one for men who visit, another for women. If my father or my brothers expected visitors, I withdrew to another room so that the men didn't catch sight of me. The only men I had spoken to until now were my father and my seven brothers. Even in my dealings with my relatives — my cousins, my uncles or my sisters' husbands — I was always extremely reserved.

Small wonder, then, that I found it exciting when this stranger rang me up. His obstinacy flattered me. Hadn't he said he liked my voice? Perhaps he had fallen in love with the sound of it. That had happened between a man and a woman in an Egyptian television series.

Who was he, and how had he got hold of my number? A day before, my younger brother Yassir had borrowed my phone. Could it be that Yassir had given one of his friends my number, and he was now ringing me up? Would my brother be as careless as that? I had heard of cases in which young men played a joke by secretly recording the voice of a woman they had illicitly telephoned. That's extremely dangerous for the woman: the caller could blackmail them with the recording at any time. It's like owning a naked photograph of her. Such proof of premarital contact can send wedding plans up in smoke and lead to divorce.

In spite of this risk, in the end I couldn't resist temptation. When my mobile lit up again just before midnight, I pressed the green button. I tried to make my voice sound strict and seductive at the same time. "What's going on?" I challenged the stranger. "How dare you terrorize us like this?"

He was probably a little surprised. Before he could reply, I said, "Please stop this nonsense," and ended the call. But of course he called again about a minute later. And of course I went back to the phone.

"What do you want?" I asked him angrily.

"I just want to talk to you," he pleaded. "Please!"

"Who are you, anyway?"

"My name is Raif Badawi."

While by now the whole world knows who Raif Badawi is, at the time, of course, the name didn't mean a thing to me. But that was about to change. Raif took my question as a challenge and, without being asked, started telling me his life story.

Raif was eighteen, and originally came from the Ha'il region in the northwest of the country. He had lived in both Riyadh and Jeddah, then in Al Khamis, and last of all here in my home town of Jizan, right in the south. He lived with a friend, and owned a share in his construction company. The two of them bought and renovated houses, before selling them on at a profit. Clearly this friend, Turad, was an acquaintance of my brother. And as they all used each other's phones all the time, the names had probably got muddled up.

I listened with fascination to Raif as he lifted the curtain on this strange world: the world of men, who were allowed to travel around independently, work and in his case even move away from home. For me, as a woman, that was completely unimaginable. And I liked the sound of his voice, speaking to me kindly and gently.

In response to his questions I too started talking about myself. I told him my name, revealed who my father was and where my family lived. Somehow I just had to take the risk.

As our phone call is a criminal act in Saudi terms, I was terrified of being caught. At the slightest sound I broke off our conversation. "Shhh, one moment," I whispered, hid the phone under my pillow and held my breath. Was someone listening at the door of my room? Was my mother about to come in? But luckily every time it was a false alarm.

Apart from those interruptions we talked all night. About the things we liked best, our inclinations and our favorite music. I told him I liked the love songs of the Egyptian singer Oum Kalthoum. Raif knew immediately what I meant. He loved the diva as well. He particularly liked "Sirat al hob"—the way of love. My favorite song was "Al hob koloh"—all the love. Raif asked me to sing him the song. He claimed not to know it, which I believed for no more than a second. None the less, I played along: I would sing if he sang too. Raif gulped, he hadn't expected this. After he had recovered from his alarm, he asked me to start.

I actually did: I pulled the covers over my head and started singing quietly for Raif, intoning in the style of the great performer. In my most seductive voice I breathed in his ear that all my love had only ever belonged to him.

Raif was completely entranced. But now I insisted that it was his turn. Raif is rather shy. So it was difficult for him, and he didn't really sing. But he recited the lyrics. He knew the words of his favorite song by heart, and spoke them as if they were a poem.

When I heard him swearing eternal love to me, describing to me how I had remade his world, and saying he would wait for me as long as he lived, I lost my heart.

We didn't say goodbye until the birds started twittering outside. And as soon as I woke up in the morning Raif called me again. After that first night together we had no doubt. The two of us belonged together.

I spent the next few days on a big pink cloud. Outwardly I

went through my normal daily business. As always I watered the roses in the back garden, flicked through my fashion magazines, helped my mother cook, served my father his lemonade in his office, met my school friend Wahiba for tea at home in the afternoon, and ordered a romper suit from the tailor for my sister's baby. But everything suddenly felt different: the roses smelled sweeter, the colors were brighter than usual. I looked at the fashion models according to whether Raif would like them. And always, constantly, I was thinking about Raif. RAIF—in Arabic it means "the sympathetic one." That matched the gentle voice on the phone.

Of course texts and phone calls soon weren't enough. Raif was determined to know what I looked like, and unfortunately our phones didn't have cameras. Meeting up was of course completely unthinkable. So we made other plans. At the time I was living with my family in a big, three-story house in the center of Jizan. My three older sisters had already married, but often visited us. Of my seven brothers the younger ones still lived at home. And my father had married twice more after my mother. He divorced his second wife so quickly that I barely got to know her. But the third one and her little children lived very near us, in the back part of the house. On the ground floor was his furniture shop. So people were constantly coming and going and you were never really alone.

Like all the women's rooms, mine faced away from the street. No one could see in from outside. My brothers' rooms, on the other hand, faced the front. In my brother Yassir's room there was a window that looked out onto the street, and the lower half of it was decorated with wooden arabesques which made it difficult, but not impossible for curious neighbors to peer in. If I wanted to show myself to Raif, it would have to be from that room.

The appropriate opportunity came one Friday. When I saw that my two brothers Yassir and Adil were leaving our house for the mosque, I sent Raif a text: "Are you nearby?" He answered straightaway. "I'll be standing in front of your house in five minutes."

"Please, Allah, don't let us get caught!" I prayed to heaven. Even though Allah was more likely to be on my father and my brothers' side. I feverishly looked for excuses in case Yassir came home early. But I couldn't think of anything convincing. I was simply insane, taking such a risk!

And my phone rang. It was Raif, of course. "I'm nearly there," he announced cheerfully.

I glanced critically at my reflection in the mirror: I was wearing a long, flowing dress. My hair was tied up at the back. I had taken my glasses off so that my profile would be prettier. Would he like me at all?

"I'm just turning into your street," he said on the phone.

"OK, then I'll come to the front of the house," I promised, sounding cooler than I felt.

I took a flower from a bunch of red carnations that my school friend Wahiba had brought the previous day. When I went into Yassir's room I could already hear the sounds of a car parking in front of our house. Raif's car? My heart turned somersaults at the thought.

He got out and vigorously closed the door. Now he was standing right in front of our house, staring up. Because of the arabesques that ran across the windowpane, and because of my shortsightedness, I could only make him out vaguely: a young man with a slight build and shoulder-length black hair. "Where are you?" his voice asked from the phone.

I stepped shyly toward the window so that at least my head was visible from below. "Is that you?" asked Raif. "Is that really you? You look stunning!"

"You can't even see me properly!"

"No, I can see that you have beautiful eyes," he stated boldly.

Whether it was true or not, I liked it. I opened the window and threw the carnation down to him. Raif picked the flower up, smelled it and hid it quickly in his jacket pocket.

"Thank you, my darling," he said raptly. "I will carry it with me always."

I hastily closed the window. "Now drive off again," I urged.

"Yes, of course…" He gave me one last, yearning look before getting into his car again and turning on the engine.

"Ensaf, do be careful!" my mother snapped when I spilled the marinade that was meant for the chicken legs on the table. Since we'd seen each other I was all over the place. My poor mother, who had firmly planned to teach me how to cook before I got married, complained bitterly — "What's up with you lately?" — and handed me a cloth to get rid of the mess. "Do you think you'll ever get a husband if you can't even cook?"

Raif and I were completely mad about one another. That was what was up. We must have spent several hours a day on the phone at that time. If we couldn't talk for some reason, we sent each other texts full of hearts, flowers and *I love you* stickers. I was totally fixated on my mobile phone: as soon as it made a sound, I pounced on it to read Raif's message. It couldn't stay hidden from my family, either. My sisters gave each other eloquent looks when they observed me. Hanan in particular, who was heavily pregnant at the time, wanted to know what was going on. And in a way she was right. After all, she had given me the phone.

After the birth of her first son, Hanan moved back in with us for a little while. Tradition demanded that my mother and we, her sisters, should look after her while she recovered from her exertions. We also set up a room for her so that she could receive well-wishers. So there was even more of a hubbub in the house than usual. But eventually Hanan and Mariam managed to find me alone in that room. "Why are you always looking at your phone?"

I fidgeted around. "Come on, out with it," said Hanan. "You can't pull the wool over our eyes."

After carrying my secret around with me for several weeks, I was ripe for a confession. And I trusted my sisters. So I told them everything.

They hung on my every word. "And when will he ask Father for your hand?" Hanan was keen to know.

"We haven't talked about that yet."

Mariam, who was older, frowned. "Just be careful," she warned me. "You know your reputation's at stake." I think she saw it as her duty to bring me to my senses. Otherwise it would fall back on her, if she was revealed to have been an accomplice. So she looked me severely in the eyes and said: "If Father finds out about this, he'll kill you."

Once that had been established, they both subjected me

to a cross-examination. They wanted to know who Raif was, what job he did, what city he came from, how many brothers and sisters he had, what position his family held. I answered to the best of my knowledge. But I could tell even by my sisters' reactions the difficulties that lay ahead. There were a few things in Raif's life that my family would find unsettling: the fact that he lived with a friend because he had had a row with his father, for example. In our society that's very unusual. So might it be better to say in future that he lived with his uncle?

"I'd so love to meet him one day," I said.

They looked at me in horror. "Don't do anything stupid!" Mariam warned me. "You'd ruin yourself and our family."

I looked guiltily at the floor. "I'd just like to see him properly so that I can be sure that I love him…Not alone, of course…" I saw them exchanging glances. "Of course," I added, "you would both have to be there."

"How do you imagine that might happen?" Hanan turned on me.

"Couldn't you invite him to your house?" I knew that Hanan's flat was empty during the day: her husband worked, the baby slept. "Just a short meeting…"

"Absolutely not," she replied categorically. But her voice suggested something else. It told me that Hanan was just as curious as I was. She looked at Mariam for support.

"Out of the question," my elder sister confirmed. "Hanan can't just let a strange man into the house. What would we say if her husband suddenly came home? Have you thought of that?"

"Only five minutes," I begged.

"You're so selfish," Mariam chided me. "Get that idea right out of your head."

I pulled a moue. But I understood my sisters: they were afraid of doing something wrong, and thus drawing the wrath of our parents or their husbands. I had to accept that. At least I would have to give them some time before trying again.

When I told Raif about it on the phone, he went completely crazy. "If I'm able to look you in the eye only once, I will shower you with flowers and jewels," he promised. I told him he would have to be patient. "If it has to be," he said, "I will wait for that moment my whole life long."

About a week later Hanan moved back with her baby to her own flat in an apartment building. Mariam and I went with her and helped her to settle in. Mariam's Filipino maid and her two little children were there too. It seemed to me to be a good opportunity to try again. "Raif would like to give me a present," I said, looking as innocent as possible. "Do you think he might bring it here, Hanan?"

She looked at me suspiciously. "Didn't we talk about this before?"

"It's just because he's nearby..."

"He can't come to my house under any circumstances."

"Not even to the door?"

Hanan looked uncertain. Part of her, the old, unmarried Hanan, couldn't imagine anything more exciting than getting a glimpse of her sister's heartthrob. Another part, the wife and mother, thought it was too risky. "What do you think?" she said, turning to Mariam.

Mariam didn't say anything for a while. Then she decided. "He's supposed to be bringing a present — and leaving straightaway."

Hanan said she agreed, even though she didn't exactly

look delighted. "But if anything goes wrong, it was Mariam who allowed it," she clarified, "and not me."

I beamed. "Nothing will go wrong," I promised.

I texted Raif the good news—and told him Hanan's address. He called me straightaway. To escape the eyes and ears of my sisters, I darted into the bathroom with my phone.

"Is that really true?" he asked in disbelief. "Can I see you?"

"Yes," I whispered, "Come quickly, before they change their minds…"

"I'll be with you straightaway, my darling!" he promised. "In a quarter of an hour."

It was the longest quarter of an hour in my life. And I spent all of it in the bathroom. Even today I remember very clearly what I was wearing that day: a tight, white blouse with almost transparent sleeves and white baggy trousers which—in line with European fashion—I allowed to slip to below my hips. I had bought the outfit shortly before in the new shopping center. It was quite risqué and sexy. But that was exactly how I wanted to present myself to Raif.

My sisters eyed me critically. "Don't you think you should perhaps wear a thin veil?" Mariam asked when I came out of the bathroom in that outfit.

"Why?" I replied. Why should I greet my beloved in a hijab? My long, dark curls were held up in a clasp. Surely that was enough. What we planned to do was so forbidden anyway that such a detail didn't count for much.

I gave a start when I heard the bell. Raif was already standing at the door. My sisters were so excited that they broke into a fit of hysterical giggles. "Open the door!" Hanan urged, and nudged me toward the hall. Mariam dragged Hanan with her into one of the back rooms. I was surprised:

she really wanted to leave me alone with Raif! She just left the door open a crack behind me. From there my sisters had a view of everything.

Tensely, I walked to the door and opened it. There stood Raif—looking completely different to how I had imagined him after glimpsing him from a distance and without my glasses. In front of me I saw a delicate, not especially tall man with relatively light skin, black hair, full lips and pitch-black eyes. I couldn't say whether the man I had imagined was more or less attractive. My fantasy figure had been handsome—and the real Raif was handsome too. But he was totally different. That was why I found it difficult to recognize him as the person I had already had the most intimate conversations with. Only his voice was familiar to me.

Raif was even more intimidated than I was. He had no idea what to say or do, but just stared at me. "You're so beautiful," he stammered, "exactly as I imagined you..." Well, that was something at least.

"Thanks," I replied in embarrassment.

Then we escaped into the ritual of handing over presents. He spread his gifts out in front of me: a chain with a purple gemstone as a pendant. And in matching color, a bracelet, earrings and a ring for my finger as well. He had also bought me some trousers: a white pair, a brown pair and a lilac pair. All far too big. But I reassured him that I could have them altered at the tailor's.

When the handover was complete, he stepped toward me. He probably wanted to give me a hug. But I recoiled instinctively. At that moment I became aware of Mariam tugging at my sleeve from the crack in the door. "Stop now," she hissed, "that's enough!" I blushed to my roots.

"I think you'd better go," I said to Raif.

"Yes, of course. I didn't know…" He broke off. "I was about to go anyway."

"Thank you very much for the presents. They're lovely. You've caught my taste exactly," I said woodenly as I ushered him from the house.

As soon as Raif was out of the door, my sisters charged over to me. They immediately wanted to see the presents. They were both very impressed by Raif. "He's really very cute," Hanan had to admit. "And charming. Just look at all the things he's brought you!"

Mariam encouraged me too. "Go the whole way," she said. "Marry him."

Easy for her to say.


During Ramadan I often slept till midday. I didn't see the point in getting up any earlier. Why should I drag myself through the day, only ever thinking about eating, when I wasn't allowed anything until the evening? It made much more strategic sense just to cut the waiting time. A lot of people do that.

Then, at sunset, it was suddenly very cozy at home. The intoxicating smell of a warm meal wafted from the kitchen, which my mother had strictly guarded all day. My favorite was the thick, oily noodle soup with a hint of peppermint that she normally served at the beginning of the fast-breaking. For me it marked the return of life to our houses. Because during Ramadan we only really lived at night. By day we just waited.

One evening shortly after the end of Ramadan, my mother came into my room, wearing an expression that did not bode well. "Your father's sent me," she said irritably. I had heard them arguing in the kitchen a little while before. Since my father had founded his new family a few years ago, the atmosphere at home was often tense. But this time it plainly wasn't about the painful theme of jealousy.

My mother didn't beat around the bush. "Do you know someone called Raif Badawi?" she demanded to know. I blushed to my roots. It was slowly becoming a habit.

"Raif?" I stammered. "Erm, never heard of him..."

"Excuse me, then, but how has this man happened on the idea of asking for your hand in marriage?" she screeched. "Can you explain that to me?"

"How should I know? Who is he anyway?"

"You know very well who he is."

"I don't!"

"Don't lie." She gave me a sound clip around the ear. I started crying.

"Shut up! Crying won't help you," she said furiously. "Give me your mobile phone right now!"

"Why?"

"Because I want it." She stretched out a hand. I gripped the phone with both of mine. I thought with horror of all the loving texts that Raif and I had sent back and forth. All the long calls that were neatly stored in the phone. My mobile was bound to give me away.

"If you don't hand it over yourself I'm sending Yassir," my mother threatened. She swept from the room. About two minutes later—I had just enough time to highlight all my texts—I heard my brother coming upstairs. With trembling fingers I pressed "delete" and stuffed my phone in between my bed and the mattress. My seventeen-year-old brother was already standing in the room. "Give me the phone, Ensaf," he said pleadingly.

"Why should I? What has it got to do with you anyway?" I flashed my eyes furiously at Yassir, but he wouldn't give in. "Just stop this nonsense," he warned me. "Father is really angry..."

Yassir looked around the room. "So, what's it to be?" he asked. "Are you going to hand it over voluntarily? Or do I have to turn the place upside down?" I didn't reply. I watched in silence as he opened the door of my clothes cupboard and looked in all the drawers. I tried to pretend I wasn't bothered, while inwardly I was clenching my fists with rage. Unconcerned, he inspected my bedside table and the chest of drawers. He rummaged through the drawers where I kept my underwear. When he asked me to get up, I stuck out my bottom lip. But I obeyed. Yassir lifted first the bedcover, then the mattress. In the gap was the phone.

"Just take it away. I don't need it anyway," I said defiantly.

"You should be ashamed of yourself, Ensaf. You're sullying our family's honor," my brother answered. He took the phone and disappeared from the room.

I didn't collapse until I was alone again. Sobbing, I lay down and pulled the covers over my head. I found it particularly depressing not even to be able to tell Raif what had happened.

My portal to the world had closed again.

Of course I knew about Raif's conversation with my father. After two months of obsessive secrecy we had decided to become a couple officially at last. But for that to happen my father had to give his agreement. In patriarchal Saudi society there is no way around that. Because in our country, until she gets married, by law the father is the guardian of the woman, regardless of how old she is. After that her husband assumes the role. If her husband dies, her father is in charge again. Or some other male relation, one of her brothers, for example, or even her son, even if he is still a minor. A Saudi woman is never her own ruler. And the men who define her life look on her more or less as their property. As I had grown up in that system, at the time I didn't question it. I was just determined to switch from my father's control to that of Raif, whom I loved. That was why I had encouraged Raif to take charge of things.

The end of Ramadan struck him as an ideal time to do just that. During Eid, the Sweet Festival, people are particularly sociable. My father always moves some furniture from his shop into the street — and welcomes friends and acquaintances for long, cordial conversations with a glass of tea and cakes.

Normally suitors go and see the bride's father with a large entourage. "He came with so many relatives that they didn't all fit into the house"; that was what people liked to say after such a visit, because the size of the group expresses the power and influence of the bride's future family. Raif couldn't provide that: as his family lived a long way from Jizan, the only person he had by his side was his business partner, Turad. In order to look more serious, Turad presented himself as Raif's uncle. Raif said straightaway that his father, with whom he had been on hostile terms since childhood, had passed away some time ago. Understandably, my father found all of this neither serious nor attractive.

He said neither yes nor no to Raif. Neither did he ask him any questions about who he was, what he did in his life and how he knew me. Worse than that: he said nothing at all. He simply ignored Raif completely. Even though several witnesses were standing around them, he pretended Raif didn't exist. Translated, his silence meant: "I'm not even going to talk about my daughter to people like you. You are not worthy of my family." It was the worst possible reaction.

When Raif told me about it on the phone I knew that we had a fight ahead of us if we wanted to have our way. He had a more optimistic outlook. "Your father just needs time to get to know me better," he thought, "then he'll change his mind."

Raif planned to make friends with my brothers so that they would put in a good word for him at his next attempt. What would he say if I told him how Yassir had just behaved? I hoped that now that the phone had gone he wouldn't write me any more revealing messages. When my family understood how intimate our relationship had become, I was pessimistic on behalf of both of us: my father was seething with rage. He and my brothers felt that their honor had already been sufficiently insulted by our secret relationship.

I went on to become a prisoner in my parents' house. I never got my phone back. I wasn't even able to use the landline unchecked. And all excursions outside of the house were strictly monitored by my brothers.

My elder sisters Mariam and Hanan, who had initially supported me in my romantic liaison, now tried to persuade me to give the whole thing up: my father would never accept Raif as a son-in-law. Our secret relationship had disqualified him once and for all. But I wouldn't hear of it. "You're talking to me like that because you've never really been in love," I barked at them. In fact, however, I wasn't half as strong as I tried to look in front of them: at that time I was boundlessly lonely, unable as I was to have any contact with Raif.

But I did find one possible way of communicating with him, through my youngest sister Hanan, who came to see us with her baby. When no one else was in the room I bewailed my suffering — and complained about my parents' limitless injustice.

"So what do you plan to do now?" she asked me, when I had finished. She really seemed to be moved by my story. Like so many women who had married in line with their parents' ideas, she herself was neither happy nor unhappy with her marriage. But she was very familiar with romantic love from the television. So she was impressed with how Raif supported our love in the face of all opposition. She also thought he was nice.

"I love him and I'm going to marry him," I said resolutely. "Whatever it takes…"

She nodded respectfully.

"Hanan, could you do me a favor?"

"What?" she asked, slightly nervously.

"Could you call Raif for me and tell him what's happened?"

"Are you crazy? Father will kill me if he finds out I'm talking to him behind his back!"

"I just want him to stop trying to call me."

Hanan got that. And it also struck her as morally inoffensive. She jotted down Raif's number and promised me she would call him as soon as she was home. "I'll explain everything to him and tell him not to call you for the time being," she said.

I waited impatiently for Hanan's next visit. While we sat with our mother in the sitting room and drank tea, she looked very mysterious. I think she enjoyed prolonging my torment and being part of our romance.

I ambushed her when we were alone at last. "Have you talked to him?"

"Yes," she smiled conspiratorially. "Several times."

"And what does he say?"

"He sends greetings. And says he loves you. And that you're not to give up hope."

My eyes filled with tears.

"Be patient for a bit, sister darling. It'll all turn out fine," she comforted me.

Over the grueling weeks that followed, Hanan became our loyal messenger. Raif would call her regularly — and then Hanan would call our house on a second phone that she had at home. Sometimes, when the situation permitted, she even allowed me and Raif a conference call, holding the two receivers together: then I could hear Raif's voice, if only from a distance.

One Friday, a month or two after Yassir had blocked direct communication between me and Raif, Hanan called us with excitement in her voice. "Are you alone, Ensaf?" she whispered.

"Yes, why?"

"Raif just called. He's on his way to your place…"

"What?" For a moment I thought she was pulling my leg. But Hanan was seriously alarmed.

"I tried to talk him out of it," she said excitedly. "But he wouldn't listen. He wants to drop off a present for you."

"Has he lost his mind?"

"He says you've got to look out the front door in five minutes."

My heart was racing. I didn't know whether to be shocked or delighted. Was it possible that Raif was already very close by? Should I go to Yassir's room and try to catch a glimpse of him? No, that was definitely too risky. My brother and my father might come back from the mosque at any time.

I decided not to do anything for the time being. Feeling tense, I sat by the phone and listened to the sounds around our house. Wasn't that the sound of a car being parked? I held my breath until I heard the car driving off again. A minute later my sister called again. "It's outside the front door," she said. "Come on, hurry up!"

I hastily pulled on my abaya. I opened the front door and looked around. There was no sign of anyone in the street. To the side of the door was an unremarkable looking parcel. I hastily grabbed it and ran up to the first floor with it.

When I opened the parcel in the safety of my room, I could hardly believe my eyes. It was a brand new mobile phone, a Baby Nokia. And a SIM card and a battery. But no personal message. Presumably Raif had been afraid that the package might fall into the wrong hands. I frantically read the instructions and put it all together. I discovered that the phone had already been set up. His number was programmed in.

I pressed the green button. "Thanks," I whispered. "How did you do that?"

He laughed. "At last I can hear your voice again, my beloved."

"You're crazy."

"No, I'm just in love with you."

"I love you too."

We swore to one another that we would allow no one and nothing to tear us apart. "I promise you I'll manage to win your family's trust," he said.

"And I'll never marry anyone else. My parents can do what they like!"

When I met my mother in the sitting room later on I tried not to look too cheerful, keen not to give myself away. I set the new phone to silent and hid it under the big built-in shelf in my room, which was directly connected to my bed. Luckily there was a plug there, so that I could hide the cable to charge it. I decided only to take it out at night, to talk to my beloved. We had to be very careful.

In the meantime Raif did everything he could to get closer to my father. He tried to spend time near his shop, and even befriended my brothers. Particularly Anwar, who is a year younger than me and three years older than Raif. He often lent Anwar his car. Anwar liked that of course. In return Raif hoped my brother would put in a good word for him with my father. He wanted to lose the stigma of being a stranger, and win a position of trust in the family.

But my father ignored him completely. He refused to meet Raif under any circumstances, and didn't even think it necessary to give him a formal answer to his marriage proposal. I think he was too preoccupied with his new wife and her family at the time. That was why he only paid halfhearted attention to what we were doing. That was particularly problematic for my mother and me, because he was our legal guardian.

The situation came to a crisis for me when I noticed that Raif had lost hope. He expressed his discouragement more and more often. When he admitted to me on the phone, "There's no point even trying with him. Your father just pretends I'm not there," I knew I would have to find a way out if I didn't want to lose him.

If my father, for whatever reason, failed to perform his duties as guardian, my brothers had to assume the task. My eldest brothers, Mohammed and Khaled, had the most authority within our family. As they had already married and no longer lived in the house, I normally had little to do with them. When they came to visit, they spent most of their time in the men's living room. But there was a way to them, and it led via my sister-in-law Ashwaq.

Just to get it out of the way, my brother Mohammed's wife is a formidable woman. She orders everyone in her immediate environment around, and since her baby died on a pilgrimage to Mecca, she has pursued religious aspirations. But my brother loves her. In fact he's devoted to her. If she said Coca-Cola wasn't black, but white, Mohammed would believe her. He's completely under her thumb. This woman, it was suddenly clear to me, could open all kinds of doors to me if she wanted to. I just had to get her on my side.

So I adopted a strategic approach. First I tried to become Ashwaq's friend. That wasn't particularly difficult: she likes people who agree with her. So that's what I did. I flattered her and reinforced her views. Once we had a fairly close relationship I started introducing her to my secrets and sharing my intimate concerns with her. Things that women like talking about. I told her about my great love, about my father's hardheartedness and our fading hope of happiness.

In spite of all the romance, this was a bit much for Ashwaq. She is a strict Muslim, you can't watch satellite television or listen to music in her house. And in the street she only ever appears clad from head to toe in black, complete with eye-veil and gloves. On the other hand Ashwaq is only a woman. And like all women she has a weakness for love stories. That was why she couldn't close herself off emotionally from my point of view, even if it struck her as morally reprehensible.

She looked at me sympathetically. "I'll put in a good word for you with your brother," she promised.

It was exactly what I wanted to hear. "Thank you," I said from the depths of my heart.

And then I brought out my strongest argument, which I had saved for the end: "You know, I'm really worried that I might do something forbidden out of sheer despair."

She looked at me in alarm. "Heaven forbid! It would bring your family into disrepute."

I nodded in contentment. Ashwaq had understood my implicit threat.

Over the next few months we played Chinese whispers at home: I wept on Ashwaq's shoulder, she worked on Mohammed. He in turn talked to my father and tried to bring him around. The argument that I would cause a scandal if I ran away with Raif was a powerful one: that wouldn't be in anyone's interest.

Everybody knew that I was still in contact with Raif in one way or another — even if they didn't understand exactly how I managed to do it in spite of all the security measures. Sometimes my brothers took my whole room apart to find the phone that they suspected was hidden somewhere in there. When that happened I hid it in my underwear. Once the vibrating alert went off when they were on one of those missions; the phone rattled away like mad in my trouser pocket.

I drew my knee up and had to summon all my strength not to burst into hysterical laughter.

Eventually they worked out that I was carrying the phone on my body. "OK, let's have the thing," my brother Mohammed demanded. "I know exactly where you've hidden the phone!"

"Really? Then come and get it. Go on, search me," I replied undaunted. I had just been to the toilet and left the phone on the windowsill, so I had nothing to fear from a body search.

Of course I didn't always emerge victorious from these little battles. My brothers caught me with the phone four times in all, and each time they took it from me. But every time Raif replaced it in the same tried and tested way. Our relationship was indestructible. It annoyed them terribly. But, stubborn as we were, Raif and I wanted to say: We're not going to give up! We insist on getting married.

Luckily, at the time we hadn't guessed that our battle was only a kind of rehearsal for the battle for Raif's life.

One evening my brother Mohammed came to my room. I was already in my pajamas. As I feared another inspection, I immediately looked around for my phone. But this time Mohammed seemed to have something quite different in mind. He was carrying a big book and sat down with it on the edge of the bed.

"Could you please sign here?" he asked, after he had opened the book.

"What is it?"

"It's the Milka document." That's the name of the register office in our country. It was about my marriage contract. I almost fainted with surprise and joy. Was it really possible? Had Raif and I prevailed? Had we attained our goal?

I could hardly have dared to hope as much. Because just before, there had been renewed dissension at our house. Since my father consistently refused to see Raif, my beloved had asked my brothers Khaled and Mohammed for an official date for an engagement, and had brought it about with the help of my sister-in-law Ashwaq. But none of the men invited to the ceremony were particularly sympathetic to his intention. So the engagement party waited in the lower rooms of our house. But my father didn't even bother to turn up. That was hugely embarrassing for everyone involved. At the time I stayed, as I always did, upstairs. On the stairs I could hear my parents arguing. "Go downstairs, will you, everyone's waiting for you," my mother scolded.

"And see that common good-for-nothing? Why should I?" my father replied.

"Because otherwise you're leaving our sons high and dry! What will people think?"

"I couldn't care less."

"You don't care about anything! And if Ensaf runs off with that fellow, you won't care about that either. Let her marry him, for heaven's sake!"

But my father remained stubborn. He didn't go downstairs. He stuck to his guns: he wasn't going to say anything at all on the subject. Meanwhile my brothers were concerned to avoid a scandal: after a year of arguments and what had become open discussion about my love affair, it was my father's attitude that threatened the honor of the family. They wanted to clarify matters before anything really serious happened and the reputations of their own families were damaged.

In the end Mohammed performed the engagement ceremony. But no one knew whether it was valid in the circumstances. That was why I was so surprised when he turned up a few weeks later with the official marriage document. With trembling hands I picked up the ballpoint pen that Mohammed held out to me and signed the paper.

"Congratulations," he said curtly.

"Thank you," I replied in confusion. Was that all? It felt completely unreal.

The signing of the marriage contract is normally a solemn act in our country. I had a father and seven brothers who were supposed to be present as witnesses. But only one had come. The rest didn't even think it necessary to congratulate me. That gave the whole business a stale aftertaste. I wanted to cheer and cry at the same time. Still, I said to myself, Raif and I had done it now.

But my family didn't think of taking the usual route from here. In the months between the Milka and the official wedding party Raif and I were only allowed to see each other one single time. My brother Mohammed invited us to his house, and we met in his living room. It is furnished in the traditional style with colorful carpets and floor cushions. Raif was wearing the traditional white garment worn by men. He came in through the guest door and sat down on the floor next to it. I entered the room from the other side, the side for family members. I wore a brown cotton blouse with an African pattern and long sleeves. I had blow-dried my long, dark hair into a flowing wave.

Raif just stared at me when I sat down on the other side of the room. I think his first impulse was to dash toward me and hug me. But I was so cool that he lost his courage and paused mid-movement.

"Hello," he said shyly. "Come a bit closer."

"Come closer yourself!" I replied cheekily.

It was a very tense situation, because my brother Khaled was constantly going in and out. He acted as our respectability guard dog — and he did his job very thoroughly. We didn't feel unobserved for a moment. Even though we normally talked for hours on the phone, at that moment it was hard for us to find a shared topic of conversation. Again we took refuge in the formalities of exchanging presents. Tradition demanded that Raif should bring me gold jewelry. In former times expensive jewelry was probably a kind of insurance for the wife, in case her husband died or something went wrong with the marriage. Raif brought me a gold ring, linked to a bracelet by a chain. I put it on my right hand. The right side represents betrothal.

"Do you like it?" he asked. I nodded shyly. I could sense it very clearly: he would have given anything to hug me at that moment. But in these surroundings that was impossible. So instead we fell back into a tense silence. After about a quarter of an hour the whole thing started to get too much for me. "Why don't we meet another time?" I suggested. "I don't really feel at ease here."

"No problem, Ensaf," he said, sadly but sympathetically. "I'll yearn for the moment when I can hold you in my arms at last, undisturbed."

We had to wait a whole six months for that moment. That was how long preparations took for the official wedding feast, for which the bride's family is traditionally responsible. And of course my family weren't in a hurry.

As in the previous few months, my brothers kept Raif waiting. The feast required careful planning, they said — and they kept putting Raif off with later and later dates. If he sent me sweets or anything they said, "What's going on? Can't you wait? Soon she'll belong to you!" As primitive as it may sound, I think it was their last chance to take revenge after losing out to him in the argument. Raif really took enormous trouble with me and with them, but the feeling of not being quite welcome in my family wounded him deeply.

But eventually even my brothers couldn't come up with any more excuses, and the wedding day was fixed once and for all. We had hired the wedding room in the Soal Hotel, one of the best places in the city, and invited 350 guests. I was content: my wedding to Raif would be held in an appropriate setting.

In the Arab world wedding feasts are largely a matter for women. Men have only walk-on parts. I too had invited only women to my wedding. We began the two-day party with a henna evening: over soft drinks and delicious snacks we painted each other's hands and feet.

My sister Hanan covered my arms with a skilful, swirling pattern. "Are you excited?" she asked me. I understood that she was referring to the wedding night.

"Not at all," I claimed. "After all, I've been waiting for almost a year and a half."

"It's not so bad. Particularly with a good-looking man like your Raif..." She giggled.

"I'm sure he can't wait," Mariam joined in.

"He's talked of nothing else for weeks," I confided to them.

Then, on the second evening, the climax of the party came, the Sefar. Until then we women had stayed among ourselves. We had talked, eaten and drunk, listened to a singer performing and danced with each other. But now, just before midnight, the ladies quickly veiled themselves: glitter and evening dresses disappeared under the black abayas. It was the moment when the men would join the party.

Our male relatives, Raif's and mine, stood at the door waiting to accompany the bridal couple as they processed into the hall. Raif wore a fine black silk gown. I was dressed all in white, like the women in foreign films. I had also powdered my face a chalky white, so the contrast with my dark hair and my red-painted lips was particularly striking. The women whistled and trilled when they saw us.

We just stood there for a while and let them cheer us. Meanwhile the band that we had hired for the occasion played their first song.

I gulped. It was the song that I had sung for Raif under the bedcovers during our first conversation. How had Raif engineered that?

As the second song began we moved slowly and solemnly into the hall. We sat down on a sofa decorated with lots of flowers, which stood on a pedestal at the end of the hall, the *kursi*. The men danced casually. The women sat wrapped in their veils on the benches, watching them and clapping.

When the band took a break, Raif brought out a wedding ring before the eyes of all the guests. It was the same ring that had been linked to the bracelet with a gold chain, which I had already worn after the Milka. But now Raif put it on my left hand, the hand that represents marriage. And with that we were married.

A short time later he left the hall, with all the other men. The women took their veils off again. I stayed alone on the *kursi* and accepted their congratulations. All my friends and relations came to me, brought their presents and told me how pleased they were for me.

"You did that very well," some of them whispered.

"Many congratulations, little fool. Now be happy with your Raif," my mother said.

I opened the buffet. After all the excitement I was incredibly hungry. But before I could go and get any food I had a text from Raif. "Where are you?" he asked impatiently.

"We're having the first buffet," I texted back.

"Come on, hurry up. Let the guests party on their own!"

I asked Hanan whether it was all right to abandon my wedding party. "If that's what the groom wishes," she replied with a grin.

I asked my mother to walk me outside. Raif was waiting there with Mohammed. My brand-new husband was a bundle of nerves. "There you are at last," he said, and he gripped my hand.

We had actually booked a suite in the hotel for the wedding night. But I was very keen to see the flat that Raif had set up for us. I already knew that it was directly below the one where Mohammed lived. So the four of us drove there in the car. Mohammed and my mother sat in the front seats; Raif and I were allowed to sit in the back. That was so unfamiliar that we were almost ashamed. Throughout the whole journey Raif didn't let go of my hand.

Our new, shared home was a three-room flat. Raif had taken a lot of trouble with the furniture. But at that point I couldn't really pay it proper attention. I was just glad that there was a place at last where we could close the door behind us.

He led me into the bedroom. He had spread out presents for me on the marriage bed: clothes, jewelry, perfume, posh bath oils and a prettily decorated wooden box. "Look inside," he said.

I opened the box and gasped. Inside was the red carnation that I had thrown from the window into the street at our first meeting. He had dried it and preserved it. "Yes," I thought, "we've done everything right. Our love is worth the endlessly difficult battle we have fought for it."

I sat down on the edge of the bed. Raif knelt in front of me and put his head in my lap. And then we both started crying: with exhaustion, with relief and with joy. We had survived. Everything would be fine in the end. At least that's what we thought at the time.

# CHAPTER TWO

# BENEATH THE VEILS OF
# THE PIOUS KINGDOM

I loved being married. At last I felt like a human being. At last I was able to do all the things my family had kept me from doing for so long: going out in the evening, going shopping, traveling. Raif and I had so much catching up to do. After sitting at home as a hostage for almost eighteen months, I hungered to experience things with him. I wanted to see the world.

So first we went on a long honeymoon: we spent the first week in Syria, the second in Lebanon. Even though both countries are largely Muslim, as a woman you can dress as you like, with or without a veil. In the capital cities at least, that's left up to the woman herself—and for me that was a great liberation. When I walked along the streets by Raif's side wearing jeans and a T-shirt, for the first time in my life I had the feeling of being really visible.

We visited the usual tourist attractions. First we went on excursions to the most important architectural monuments. In Syria we saw the ancient city of Palmyra, in Lebanon we went to Baalbek, which I knew from the legendary concerts of the singer Fairuz on television. I knew her ballads by heart. And now, when I walked with Raif through the romantic backdrop of the old stones, I hummed one of the songs and Raif joined in softly.

The song tells the story of a pair of secret lovers whose romance comes to light and is shattered because their love letters are discovered. How lucky we had been, now we were able to be together for ever! Back then, in the ruins of Baalbek, I thought it unimaginable that we would ever be parted again.

I really liked Lebanon, even more than Syria. Everything there is so green, you would almost think you were in France. At least that was how I imagined France because of the French films I had seen on television. We went on excursions into the mountains, where there are very pretty Christian villages. But the best of all was the night life in Beirut. We plunged into the hubbub and painted the restaurants, casinos and discos red. We had to try out every new bar, and I found everything incredibly exciting: after all, I had never gone out in the evening in my life. Let alone uncovered, in tight, short-sleeved tops.

Generally speaking, this was my time of "first times." It was the first time I'd been free and independent—without my brothers checking up on me day and night. For the first time, with my beloved, I could determine what I wanted to do. And for the first time—without a veil over my face—I had a clear view of the sky.

Raif and I got on well from the beginning. As we had already talked to each other in such detail on the phone, we weren't strangers to one another. We each knew how the other thought and felt. It was a great advantage. And it's far from ubiquitous in our culture: many couples who have been married off by their parents have to get to know one another after the wedding. And often it comes as an unpleasant surprise.

But Raif and I were just happy because we had each other, and enjoyed being together. At last we could stroll hand in hand through the bazaar without anyone taking offense. Sometimes we stole a glance at each other, and we still couldn't believe it. We were everything all at once: friend, sibling, lover, marriage partner.

Raif is an extremely attentive and generous man. He spoiled me a lot during this time. He was constantly buying me new clothes. Sometimes quite risqué things, like a western bathing costume and summer dresses that I would never be able to wear at home. But on holiday we allowed ourselves these liberties, as almost all Saudis do when they leave the kingdom and its strict rules behind.

Lest there be any misunderstanding, Raif and I weren't a very progressive couple in those days. We thought and felt exactly the same as all Saudis. Raif was rather conservative, not least in his attitude toward women. Neither of us questioned the classical division of gender roles. At the start of our marriage he was, in fact, relatively devout, and made a great effort to keep to all the religious rules, particularly the prayer times, set out by Islam.

During our last week in Lebanon I noticed that I was suddenly feeling weak and tired. When Raif suggested going out in the evening, I told him I would rather go to bed early. The next morning I felt so bad that I had to throw up in the toilet. Raif looked at me with concern. "Maybe you've caught something?" he asked, thinking it was some kind of viral infection. But I had another idea.

"Yes, perhaps..." I said ambiguously. "Come on, let's go to the chemist's." Raif thought I wanted to buy tablets for my stomach pain. He offered to collect the medicine for me. But I insisted on going with him.

"It may be that I don't need any medicine," I said. But he wouldn't hear of it. It was only when I asked for a pregnancy test at the counter that the penny dropped.

"From the first week?" the chemist asked. I looked at Raif. But he was so perplexed that he was lost for words.

"Yes," I said, and helped Raif with his wallet, so that the poor man would get his money. Then I pushed him out of the shop.

"Why didn't you tell me?" he exploded as soon as we were in the street.

"What was I supposed to tell you? I had no idea myself! It was just a suspicion."

Raif was over the moon. He insisted that we go straight back to the hotel room to take the test. While I went to the toilet with the strip, he waited outside the door. From inside I could hear him pacing up and down the room. He made me so nervous. I wet the strip. Holding my breath I stared at the test to see if it was changing color: two strips equals pregnancy, one strip equals no pregnancy. That was what it said on the packaging leaflet.

I didn't know what to hope for: Raif and I wanted children, that much was clear. It was so obvious to us that we didn't even have to talk about it. But so soon? I wondered secretly. The past two months had been the loveliest of my life. For my liking, things could have gone on like that for a while. To be honest, I wanted to have Raif to myself for a while, and enjoy my freedom.

I gave a start: was that a slight change of color on the white background? Now the outline of the second strip was becoming clearer and clearer. Yes, no doubt about it: there were two strips. I was pregnant! That had gone pretty damned quickly.

I stayed in the toilet for a few moments and breathed deeply. My life was about to change completely. Just as every woman's life changes when she has children. But that was fine. After all, the child would be Raif's. A small human being, half Raif, half me. At that thought I noticed a warm feeling flowing through my body. Our child was bound to be beautiful, I thought tenderly.

"Everything all right in there?" Raif called.

"Yes," I replied, "just a minute."

Raif waited for me just behind the door. "And?" he asked, wide-eyed.

I held the test under his nose.

"Does that mean...?"

I nodded. His eyes filled with tears. "I'm going to be a father," he murmured, deeply moved.

I could tell by his reaction that he was really delighted. He hugged me. "I've always wanted children. You're making me the happiest man in the world, Ensaf," he said. "Do you know if it's going to be a girl or a boy?"

I laughed. "Do you think I'm a clairvoyant or something?"

"If it's a girl, let's call her Najwa. After my mother," he explained solemnly. "Agreed?" He looked at me expectantly.

I knew Raif loved and revered his late mother above all else. She was Lebanese, and had been a Christian before marrying Raif's father and converting to Islam. While she was still young she developed cancer and died before Raif was ten years old. He never really got over her loss. It gapes like an open wound in his life.

"I couldn't imagine a better name," I replied.

He beamed. "Najwa, Najwa, are you in there?" he said, and tenderly touched my belly with his hand.

Raif carried the strip with the test result around in his wallet for weeks. He was absolutely delighted, and told all his friends about it. After we had been to the ultrasound clinic together, and could be sure that we were actually going to have a daughter, he started buying clothes and dolls for her. Even before Najwa was born Raif was already crazy about her.

Meanwhile we had gone back to Jizan and moved into the flat below my brother's. I enjoyed doing it up for the birth of the child, and at the same time I began developing my own ideas: I bought a crib and a changing table. I also changed all the curtains and bedclothes.

But I still didn't really feel free — or not as free as I had dreamed I might be before the wedding. That was due above all to the fact that we were under constant observation. We kept having to give my brother an account of what we were doing. If he didn't find us at home, the very next day he wanted to know where we had been.

In the evening he and his wife often invited us to dinner. Ashwaq is a great cook. She usually made traditional recipes. I returned the invitations very rarely. "Do you ever cook for your husband?" Mohammed once asked me, when he cheekily inspected my fridge and found it contained mostly Coca-Cola, Red Bull and frozen pizza.

"We prefer to go out. Raif's really fond of fast food," I answered without thinking.

"Have you ever wondered why? It's as if our mother never taught you anything," he grumbled.

"If you're going to have a baby, you should really learn to cook," added Ashwaq, who found our lifestyle equally infuriating, but was at the same time rather envious of it. "You won't be able to manage otherwise."

Reproaches like this left me fuming. Would she never leave me and Raif in peace? Mohammed and Ashwaq sometimes behaved almost as if they had been given educational responsibility for us. And perhaps in a way they had: I suspected my brothers, and also my father, of giving them this role. Raif, who had not forgotten his ill-treatment by my family before our wedding, was disturbed almost more than I was by their constant interference in our private life. It was as if they were actually waiting for something to go wrong at our house — so that they could come and give us a good scolding.

So I never complained at home. Even if Raif and I argued — which sometimes happened — no one found out about it from me. I didn't provide anyone with ammunition against us. I knew my place. And if I ever had to choose between them and him, it wouldn't be hard. Back then, heavily pregnant, I had no idea that that day would come very soon.

Shortly before the baby was born Raif revealed to me that he had to travel to Lebanon on business with his partner Turad. Turad was something like a mentor or an older brother to Raif. They claimed they had to meet an important investor in Beirut. But I suspected the two men just wanted to have a few nice days away, and that the trip wasn't strictly necessary from a business point of view. So I told Raif he had to be back before our child came into the world. He gave me his solemn promise. "It's more than two weeks away," he said. "I've worked out the date quite precisely."

Shortly after he left, I felt a sharp pain in my abdomen. I had gone into labor. And I was totally alone in the house. I felt betrayed: how could Raif have been so far out with his calculations?

I started putting some things together for the hospital. At first I was going to tell Mohammed and Ashwaq, but then I decided to call Raif instead. I was weeping with rage.

"I'll be with you straightaway, darling," he said in a placatory voice. "I'll catch the next plane to Riyadh." He sounded properly contrite. I had the feeling that he was furious with himself for getting the date wrong. He promised he would do everything he could to be with me in the hospital before the child came. His promises reassured me somewhat. Even though I wasn't sure he could keep them, it felt good to hear them.

Then my family took charge. Mohammed and Ashwaq drove me to the hospital. There my sisters looked after me. Najwa was born only a few hours later. When they laid the baby on my belly, I saw straightaway that she had her father's fine features. I was delighted. I couldn't even be annoyed with Raif.

When it was all over they brought me to my parents' house. They set up a room for me, with a little bed for the baby. As I've said, that is the custom in our country when a daughter of the house becomes a mother for the first time. Over the next few days relatives and friends come to congratulate her, bring her presents and of course admire the infant.

At last Najwa's father arrived as well. He came straight from the airport. But my family treated him like a stranger: they stopped him from going into my room. He had to wait in the visitors' room. That was something of an affront. My brother Adil told me I should greet him there.

When I came in with the baby, Raif immediately leaped to his feet and ran toward us. He kissed me and then hugged us both tenderly for a long time. Too long, my brothers thought, as they looked at us jealously.

"Couldn't you wait till you're on your own?" Adil hissed angrily.

"Really," Yassir joined in. "You'd think you had no home of your own..."

These remarks were deeply shaming to both of us. Raif looked at my brothers for a long time, without saying a word. But Najwa, who noticed that the mood had changed, started wailing. "I have to tend to the child," I apologized—and I was about to flee this uncomfortable situation when Raif held me back.

"Please pack your things, Ensaf," he said. "We're going home."

"Right now?"

"Straightaway."

I understood Raif's irritation. He couldn't put up with the way he'd been treated. The fact that my brothers couldn't stand him was one thing. But treating him with so little respect was absolutely out of the question. He was my husband, after all. Within five minutes I had marched out, taking Najwa with me.

"Think hard about what you're doing," my mother called out behind me. "What will people say?"

I didn't really care: my brothers had humiliated Raif. I had to stand by him. Their behavior forced me to break with them and side completely with Raif.

"We can't go on like this," he said when we were sitting together in the car. "I'd like us to move."

"You mean we should leave the city?" I was shocked.

"Yes," he said. "Let's move to Jeddah. We'll never be able to breathe in Jizan." He looked at me. "You've got to make your choice: your family or me."

"I've made that decision already," I reminded him, "when I married you."

He smiled — and I thought I caught a hint of a guilty conscience in his face. As if he meant: I hope you haven't started regretting it?

We kept our plans to move secret. Raif organized everything. Two weeks later we flew to Jeddah, the big port and trading city on the Red Sea, about 400 miles north of my home town.

I had been to Jeddah often. Usually passing through, when I made the pilgrimage to Mecca with my family as a child. I hadn't warmed to the metropolis. I'd always found it too big and too noisy. But Raif tried to bring me around to it: there were more foreigners there, he said. So there was a more international, liberal air to it.

OK. Everything's relative. In comparison with Jizan perhaps Jeddah really was "liberal" — meaning that women weren't completely condemned to sitting at home and twiddling their thumbs. The more affluent went strolling around the shopping malls in the afternoon. And a very few even worked. But what good was that to me? I didn't know anyone. And I didn't know how to meet anyone in that concrete desert. When did you get the opportunity to do something like that? My life so far had revolved entirely around my family.

Raif had a business plan. The construction company that he had run with Turad hadn't been going particularly well lately. So it wasn't a hard decision to sell it and reinvest the money. He wanted to move into a new and promising market: training institutes. Shortly after the turn of the millennium it had become fashionable to learn English and computer studies. Both were useful skills when it came to using the emerging Internet effectively. In particular, there was very little such training available for women. And in a metropolis like Jeddah there were a lot of people with an interest in further education: they didn't want to be left behind by the modern world. Raif recognized the enormous potential going to waste there.

So he took over the management of a private institute that taught English and computing, to women in particular. Curiously, to do that he needed my teaching permit from university: my diploma as a teacher of the Qur'an, which was valid for both of us as a couple, was his ticket to the world of education. But of course Raif didn't do any teaching himself. He managed the institute, ensured that it was running financially, placed advertisements and drummed up publicity to increase the number of students.

There was a lot of work involved at first—and Raif spent many hours in his office. But his concept soon turned out to be successful. The idea caught the spirit of the time, and more and more women students enrolled; soon there were several hundred. Raif had trouble finding enough teachers for them. He usually recruited them from other Arab states, as there were not enough qualified women in Saudi Arabia. And Saudi salaries were very attractive to foreigners.

He worked with a vice-director, who assumed responsibility for internal communication for him. As a man he wasn't even allowed to enter the spaces where the women students and teachers spent their time. The classrooms were set aside for women alone, so that they could take off their impractical abayas. The same had been true in my Qur'an school. But at Raif's institute there was a passageway from the classrooms to the administrative section which contained his office.

I played no part in this world, as I stayed at home with the baby. All I learned of it was Raif's excessive workload: he toiled away from dawn till dusk. And the gratifying effects on our bank account: soon we were materially very prosperous. Raif even engaged two maids — an Ethiopian who cleaned for us, and an Indonesian who helped me in the kitchen.

But I still felt very lonely in this strange city. I didn't speak to anyone, had no exchanges with anyone. Who could I visit when Raif went to work? I was depressed by the anonymity of the city: no one here seemed to know anyone else. Without my family I was completely isolated from social life. And Raif's family was no alternative. Admittedly his father wasn't dead, as he had initially claimed to my parents, but in retrospect I wished he had been. Raif himself had only come out with the truth about his father some time after our wedding. And it had shaken me to the core.

Mohammed Raif Badawi, or Abu Raif, as we call him, meaning "Raif's father," is a very special person. I don't want to speak ill of him, since it's very important in our culture to show respect to one's parents and particularly to one's parents-in-law. But everything I am about to say, I say with Raif's permission — and with his express approval.

So where should I start? I said at the beginning that my marriage to Raif was so complicated, and encountered so much resistance on the part of my parents, because Raif had claimed that his father was dead. My parents were furious when they discovered that it wasn't true. But in my opinion it was the best thing he could have done: anyone with such a father would rather declare him dead — because in that way he can do him the least harm. In his position I would have done exactly the same.

Raif was nine when his mother died. From that point he and his brothers and sisters were handed over to a man who was a strict disciplinarian. He can only be described as a tyrant.

His temper was worse. Raif told me that he married at least three women a year before rejecting them. And he wasn't exaggerating: a nonjudicial investigative commission from Jeddah recorded the number of his wives as fourteen. None of the wives were able to help the children. "[These women] were all afraid of my father. None of them dared to stand up to him," Raif told me.

Raif and his sister Samar tried more than once to run away from home. They sought refuge with relatives. Or they tried to survive in the streets on their own, like homeless children. "Anything was better than being at home," Raif confided to me.

When Raif's aunt, a sister of his father's, wanted to send the two runaways back home, Raif refused to go. He was just thirteen at the time. He and Samar had already tried countless times to escape the situation at home. When their father came to collect them, Raif threw himself at his aunt's feet and gripped her knee: "Please, please, let us stay with you," he pleaded.

His father became very angry. "So, the young man doesn't want to come home?" he said. "We'll see about that. Unruly boys like you have no business being at home anyway. There's a more appropriate place for them: they'll teach you discipline in prison!"

Mohammed Badawi dragged his son to the police station and accused him of "disobedience to his parents." For readers who live in a constitutional state that may sound absurd. But in Saudi Arabia it's possible for parents to level such accusations at their underage children. And disobedience is considered a serious crime.

The authorities did not take long to examine the case. As Raif's father was his son's guardian and educator, it was superfluous: he had decided to punish his son — so they complied with his wishes and locked up the thirteen-year-old.

Raif ended up in children's prison. By way of greeting, the warders first of all whipped him; in the course of his imprisonment that would happen quite often. In retrospect he describes the time that he spent in this institution as "the worst days of my life."

"Worse than what you have to put up with now?" I asked him once when he called me from prison in Kanda.

"Yes, worse, Ensaf," he said. "Don't forget: I was only thirteen years old, and helplessly exposed to those monsters. I had no idea where I would end up, what would happen to me, whether I would ever get out."

Raif was imprisoned with about 300 children of his age, all boys between six and seventeen. Many of them were locked up for crimes such as theft or the like. Only a very few had been sent by their parents.

There were bars on the windows of their dormitory. Conversations between them were strictly forbidden. Even over meals there had to be absolute silence. Anyone who infringed the rule was beaten with sticks by the guards. The blows were so hard that the boys often fainted. It was supposed to have a deterrent effect on the others.

The daily lives of the little delinquents were very tightly structured, and consisted largely of a single activity: Qur'anic studies. Talking was allowed in the classroom — but only in religious verses. "We spent almost all our time learning the Qur'an and the Hadiths by heart," Raif told me. In Saudi Arabia it's considered a panacea. "All of our teachers were incredibly religious, and constantly warned us to be humble and devout."

After a very short time they had left Raif completely intimidated. No one waited for him on the weekly visiting day. "I felt completely abandoned," he told me. "No one asked after me. No one came to visit me. But above all I didn't know if I would ever set foot outside those walls, whether I would ever see light and air again. That was actually the worst thing."

In his despair he turned to God, the only authority accessible to him. He started praying, and begged the Almighty to take pity on him. If he ever knew freedom again, he would become a respectable boy, he promised, pious and devout.

After six months his relatives came at last to collect him. Raif's father would have liked to keep his son in the institution for longer, but the elder Badawi's siblings, chiefly Raif's aunt, had pricked his conscience.

"When I left that place I was a different person," Raif told me. "I was very, very strongly religious, and took meticulous care to keep all the religious rules. Above all the prayer times. For fear of ending up in jail again, I didn't want to do anything wrong under any circumstances. I'd been subjected to some kind of brainwashing."

Raif's father found the change that his son had undergone quite positive at first: in particular, the devout trait that his tormentors had instilled in him was very much in line with his own authoritarian personality. But he didn't keep the peace for long. At the age of fourteen Raif finally managed to run away and escape for good. After that he lived with friends and relatives until we married.

I'm sure I don't need to emphasize how much this story deepened my love and sympathy for Raif. When I saw the tenderness with which he treated my daughter, and at the same time imagined what he had had to endure as a child, sometimes I was almost breathless with pain and love for Raif. But that wasn't the only aspect of him that was new to me. The second new side of my husband did not have such tragic dimensions, but it did unfortunately sometimes cause our marriage to falter.

Three months after Najwa's birth I discovered that I was pregnant again. When I told Raif, he was delighted. "We'll have a large family," he said, and kissed me. He was very fond of children. But his mind was elsewhere, I could tell quite clearly.

This time he barely paid any attention to my pregnancy. I have very bad memories of it. It put terrible strains on me, both physically and mentally. Physically, because my body had hardly had time to recover from the exertions of the first; mentally, because during this time Raif and I became estranged from one another. When he came home in the evening he was exhausted, and hardly told me anything about what he had experienced during the day. It was a source of great concern to me.

I found the situation highly paradoxical: now that we had finally left everything behind us, now all our troubles had fled and we were very comfortable financially, as a couple we suddenly had nothing left to say to each other. Before the children I had been a friend and lover to Raif, and he had fulfilled my every wish. I was — at least that was how he made me feel — the center of his world. But when I fell pregnant so quickly and gave birth to our first daughter, we both began assigning each other the traditional roles within a marriage. In retrospect I blame Saudi Arabian machismo for this. If men grow up with the idea that they make all the decisions within the family, and where possible keep women out of everything that they do outside it, it's inevitable. Eventually they come to live in different worlds.

And at the start of our marriage Raif too believed that his only task consisted in ensuring the material well-being of the family. I wasn't to take an interest in exactly how he did that. He didn't tell me about his worries or his plans, about the people he had met and what they had talked about. Our conversations revolved around subjects relating to the family, the flat and our everyday life. And Raif had the last word in all our decisions. Sometimes he didn't involve me in them at all, as for example when he thought about buying a new car. The conviction of the husband's "natural superiority," too, was deeply rooted in him. It had been dinned into him from early childhood, and confirmed time and again. How else was he supposed to think? And how else was the relationship to develop if he acted as if he had more rights than I did? So, in the course of the first two years of our marriage, our love lost the deep intimacy that had initially bound us together. We were living out the traditional Saudi Arabian gender roles. Except that I was the loser. Alone in a strange city, I lacked the female parallel cosmos that Saudi Arabian women form with their sisters and sisters-in-law within their families and extended families. Apart from my little daughter and my domestic staff I had no one I could spend the day with, let alone talk to.

Against this background I found it harder and harder to believe that Raif was building up his institute from morning till evening. It didn't fit with what I knew of him. It was fine that he should devote himself to his work, but why did he spend almost the whole of his life outside the house, basically coming home only to sleep? Why did he spend so little time with me and Najwa? Why had he stopped taking me out for dinner?

With my fat belly I felt unhappy and on the defensive. Had I stopped being desirable to Raif? The shapelessness and heaviness — and the constant hormonal surges — made me sensitive and tearful, even though I didn't want to be. I found it very hard to bear. It was as if something alien had taken hold of me. As if I was no longer the old, carefree Ensaf, as if I had turned into someone else. And there was nothing at all that I could do about it. I simply had to accept what was happening to my body.

So I yearned for the end of this pregnancy. Unconsciously, above all I blamed my physical condition for the fact that Raif was turning away from me. Once I had my normal, petite figure back, he would definitely show more interest in me again, I thought — very naively.

This time I had to make the preparations for the birth all on my own: I had no one to go shopping for romper suits with. No one I could share my anxieties with. No one I could talk to about which hospital would be best. Only my neighbor called in every now and again. We would drink tea together while she gave me a few tips. But it's quite different having your family nearby. However willingly I had followed Raif into our new life, it wasn't easy for me.

Our son was born exactly a year after our daughter. If I had hoped that his birth would bring us closer together again, I was to be sorely mistaken. It exacerbated the tensions between us. You couldn't say that Raif rejected the child. On the contrary: the fact that the child was a boy made him very happy. Sons, particularly the firstborn, are very special to Saudi men. They are seen more or less as a younger version of the father. Raif couldn't change his skin.

In the hospital he picked up the newborn baby. "I'll call you Turad," he announced. Raif was working closely with his friend and business partner again in Jeddah.

I was horrified. Turad represented the world out there, in which Raif wouldn't let me participate. He represented the part of Raif that I had lost, the one I no longer had access to. I always suspected Turad of reinforcing Raif's macho delusions, which were causing me such suffering. And that was who our son was to be called after?

I pulled a disappointed face. But Raif had already made his decision. He didn't even ask me my opinion. So I took the path of passive resistance at which Saudi women are such experts. I secretly decided simply to address the baby by another name. I thought Dodi was nice. And that was what I called him — and still call him today.

Now I had two screaming babies at home, and Raif spent most of his time elsewhere. He didn't come home until late in the evening. I usually pretended I was already asleep. In reality, however, I waited impatiently for the sound of his key in the lock, to hear him creeping on tiptoe into the bedroom that we shared. Then he would embrace me from behind with his warm hands. In spite of the estrangement between us he did that every night.

One day, Raif came back a little earlier than usual, and slumped on the couch in exhaustion. He went to sleep there straightaway. He had left his phone in the kitchen. I sometimes heard it buzzing several times in sequence. That aroused my interest. Raif was clearly getting a whole series of texts. But who was sending them?

I hesitantly approached the phone. "No, don't do it!" an inner voice warned me. "Why not? You're his wife and have a right to know," another countered. As if guided by remote control I approached the phone and tried to find the menu. But Raif had set up a locking code.

I had been tapping around on the keyboard for a while when the phone suddenly rang. Following a spontaneous impulse, I pressed the green answer button. "Hello?" I whispered, disguising my voice. "I can't talk now. Ensaf is nearby…"

"OK, OK," said the woman at the other end. "Call me later."

After I had hung up, I thought the ground was disappearing from under my feet. So it was true. I wasn't a paranoid wife, and all my moments of suspicion were justified: Raif really was having contact with another woman behind my back.

I could have thrown the phone against the wall. But now it was active — I had to exploit the fact. I quickly tapped my way into the menu before it returned to locked mode. According to the display, it was a certain Shirin who had called him. It didn't take me long to find the name in his messages. The sequence of texts that they had sent each other was like a knife through my heart. "*Habibi* — my love," it said, "I miss you…" "I would so love to meet you outside the institute once but I know this will never happen." It swarmed with smilies, hearts and other icons. In short the texts looked exactly the same as the ones that Raif and I had once sent each other. At a time when we had not even known each other. At a time when I had been ready to break with my family to follow this man wherever he wanted me to go.

I actually felt ill when I read that. Revolted, I set the phone down. Raif was still asleep. His delicate features looked calm and peaceful. Those features that I had loved more than anything. And which, damn it, I still loved. And hated at the same time. The longer I looked at him the greater the rage in me became. How could Raif do that to me? How could he sleep so soundly on our living-room couch, and the next moment send little hearts to another woman? After all we had been through. After our beautiful love story.

No, really: I no longer understood the world. What was I supposed to do now, I wondered, kill him? Or her? I'm glad I didn't have a pistol to hand at that moment. Because I'm sure I could easily have used it.

I crept around him. It was that damned institute, I was

sure of it: the institute full of women. It must have driven Raif out of his mind. How could it have been otherwise?

In Saudi Arabia men and women *can't* have normal contact with each other if they meet outside the family. As such a situation is not considered possible in our country, there is also no code of behavior, no normality. In fact the strict separation of the genders leads to an over-sexualization of the opposite sex. All that men normally get to see of women is eyeless, black mountains of fabric that look a little like Darth Vader from *Star Wars*. They simply don't have any experience of seeing unveiled women. And as soon as they catch sight of a feminine attribute — a pretty sandal, for example, with a delicate feminine foot in it — they totally freak out. Their hormones start working overtime.

It isn't very different for Saudi women: as we are constantly screened off from the men, we develop an incredible curiosity about the opposite sex. In fact I would almost go so far as to say we are starved of any kind of contact with men. And we all have various romantic films in our heads, love stories — and we dream of experiencing something like that ourselves. That's why any kind word is immediately interpreted as flirtation.

If men and women meet under such circumstances, a kind of chemical reaction takes place; there just has to be a spark. Particularly in the younger generation. Aside from prudery and piety, that's why Saudi Arabia is in my view a thoroughly sexualized country: in principle everything revolves around sex — and the question of how it can be most effectively prevented. Even the public debate is always about building new hurdles between the sexes. Curiously, of course, it has precisely the opposite effect.

Now Raif opened his eyes. I flashed my eyes furiously at him. "What's up?" he asked drowsily. "Is there something wrong?"

"Something wrong?" I hissed at him. I held his phone under his nose. Unfortunately it had by now fallen back into inactive mode. "Who's this Shirin? What does she want from you?"

"Shirin? Shirin?" Raif pretended to be struggling. He shook his head. "I don't know who you mean."

"You know very well! Why are you sending her love hearts?"

I waited for his reaction, but Raif remained silent.

"Give me an answer!"

"I don't know what you're talking about, Ensaf. Really. I think you're imagining things."

"I'm not imagining anything at all!" His brazen lies were making me angrier and angrier.

"What are you doing with my phone anyway?" Raif said, going on the counterattack. "It has absolutely nothing to do with you." He took the phone away from me.

"Oh, I think it does!"

I tried to grab the phone off him again. But he was faster than me and held my hand firmly. We were a moment away from coming to blows. "Stop this nonsense right now," he said.

"It isn't nonsense," I roared. "Who is she? Tell me the truth!"

Raif turned away. "You're crazy," he said. "I don't know any Shirin. Would you just let me get back to sleep?" He ostentatiously closed his eyes — and let my fury peter out into nothing, while I lost my mind.

I looked at him lying there like that. My beloved husband, for whom I had left almost everything in life behind me. The father of my two children, whom I had willingly followed to a strange city, and whose own father had stolen his childhood. Did he perhaps think he could pull the wool over my eyes, the bastard?

I stopped talking to him, for several days. It was a help-less gesture. As a Saudi woman you have few options, quite honestly, if your husband is making problems. Strictly speaking you have only two: I could simply put up with it — or I could complain to my parents. It is entirely customary for the family to mediate in marital disputes. Because in such disagreements the woman needs a kind of advocate to com-pensate for her weaker starting position. The role can be assumed by her father or another male relative. But I didn't want to expose myself by confiding in my family. Given the earlier conflicts between them and Raif it would have been like admitting defeat. I didn't want to do that to myself.

So I didn't say anything to anyone, not a single word. My pride sealed my lips. I didn't even hint to my sisters that things weren't right at home. During our phone calls I always pretended to be the happiest person in the world so that they could tell my parents and brothers. In fact I was very lonely, after my great love had disappointed me. No one knew how much I was suffering during that time. No one but Raif.

But he maintained his position of denying everything and saying I was mad. Raif just acted as if my claims were com-pletely empty and absurd.

Like all Saudi men he thought he had a God-given right to talk to members of the opposite sex. Just as obviously, he denied me the same right. This traditional setup had already been valid for generations of marriages within our culture. For a man it was far too comfortable to question. The same held for Raif. At least back then. He wasn't ready yet.

After what had happened he looked after his phone very carefully. He never left it lying around unguarded again. That annoyed me. Because obviously I made further investigations.

My ally — and informant — was to be the institute's chauffeur. It happened by chance. This man, Mr. Alam, sometimes came to collect me in the car to take me out: to the doctor's, to go shopping and things like that. Since I, as a woman, couldn't drive a car, and since there is no public transport in Saudi Arabia that I could have taken, I had to rely on being driven. If I had to go anywhere, I called Raif and he sent Mr. Alam along. Mr. Alam was a Bangladeshi. He was already quite old, with a gray goatee which, because of his Asian origins, never grew particularly thick, and he wore the traditional white robe with a Bengali cap on his head.

Mr. Alam is a deeply religious man, which is why he wasn't happy that Raif was so popular with women. On the way to the hairdresser one day Mr. Alam mentioned that women often visited Raif's office. He thought that was not proper. Mr. Alam could only know that because the doors to Raif's office stood always wide open — we were living in Saudi Arabia, after all.

"Oh, really?" I replied, apparently unmoved. In fact, of course, I itched to know more. Just as Mr. Alam had intended.

It is quite clear that Raif gets on well with the ladies: he is charming, kind and eloquent. And he now often had the chance to talk to them. His number was on all announcements and advertising prospectuses — so they called him if they were interested in courses. Or he met them when they came into the office to enroll. Or if they told him about problems they were having. As I say, he had plenty of opportunities.

Some of the students probably wanted to gain advantage for themselves by making eyes at him. Free lessons. Better marks. Maybe a job at the institute? I don't know exactly.

In those days I always waited for opportunities to be driven around by Mr. Alam. On the way he said nothing at all. I liked his unobtrusive manners, even though I was exploding with curiosity.

As we drove back and forth around Jeddah, I kept wondering whether I shouldn't just leave the subject alone; I condemned my own thirst for knowledge. What difference did it make whether I knew who was visiting Raif's office quite often? Should I really burden myself with the details?

But usually, as we turned off the highway just before we reached the street where our flat was, I could bear it no longer. "So?" I asked casually. "Any news from the institute?"

He immediately understood what I was getting at. "Indeed, madame," he replied eagerly. He willingly told me which woman was going particularly often to Raif's office. I took my revenge with an ample tip.

Sometimes I even went to the institute to take a look at my competitors. It was very painful to me, but before I had sleepless nights over a new flame, I preferred to see her face. I had to check her out: was she a match for me? Prettier? Did I need to have serious worries about how I stood with Raif?

Usually the sight of her was reassuring, because I didn't have a sense that I was falling short of these ladies in any respect. On the contrary. Often I could only shake my head over Raif's choices, and think: what are you doing with her, when you've got me at home? Is that really your level, Raif? Turning up at the institute was, of course, also my way of marking my territory. It signaled to everybody: I'm here! I'm the director's wife! And I'm not going to abandon that position.

Aside from Mr. Alam, there were other people at the institute who felt the need to inform me about Raif's intrigues. Various teachers came up to me and told me the latest gossip. But I snubbed them all. I knew that there were all manner of petty jealousies at the institute — and that they were all determined to blacken each other's names. So I told each of them, when they came to me with this information, that I wasn't interested. I even warned them not to spread rumors.

But I couldn't stop them. Over time, Raif actually started having serious problems because he was friendly to everyone. In Saudi Arabia educational institutions for women are kept under strict moral surveillance. There is a state examination commission that visits the establishment at regular intervals and inspects everything on the spot. Are the students correctly dressed? Is their private sphere adequately protected? Are precautions taken to ensure that men aren't allowed in the classrooms? Is the educational material suitable for women? Questions like that. Of course both the students and the staff are questioned about such matters.

And then some disappointed lady must have made a critical remark about Raif. Not right at the beginning, but after about two years. I found out through Fauzia, the Ethiopian who cleaned at our house. Her sister Rukaya cooked at the institute and picked up all kinds of tales — which Fauzia passed on to me, fresh from the rumor mill.

Raif's deputy tried to cover his back. Once she called

home and asked him not to come to the institute. The inspectors were in the building again. But even she couldn't dispel all their concerns. The inspections became more and more frequent. That in turn affected the number of new applications. But Raif didn't tell me a word about that. And neither did I mention to him that I knew about his difficulties: they were his concern. After all, he had brought about this situation himself.

It wasn't an easy time for us, but it was hardest of all for me.

I saw only one way for me to become a happy person again. I had to win Raif back. Somewhere deep inside him there had to be the old Raif, the man who had laid the world at my feet only two years before. And who had fought like a lion to be able to marry me.

I was not indifferent to this man, I knew. He still loved me too. Because when Raif loved, he loved forever. So what had happened? Perhaps, I thought, my constant presence at home meant he took me for granted. He no longer saw me as his booty—and as a consequence he no longer made an effort on my behalf.

That was going to change, I decided: I wouldn't stay at home any longer worrying about what he happened to be doing. It was making me ill. I would build up my own life. Without Raif. If he could get by without me, I'd been managing without him for ages.

We had just moved into a different flat. It was bigger and nicer than our first one. And it was in a better area. I wouldn't make the same mistake here and lock myself away at home on my own, I swore. I decided to get to know my neighbors.

My first friend was the Egyptian Lania, who lived in

the same block, a few floors below us. I bumped into her by chance in the lift one day. As she was a foreigner, she didn't have any family either, and was trying to make contact with other women to distract herself a little. She introduced me to some of the other women she'd met. We were all united by the same fate: we had husbands who earned a lot, but we spent far too much time sitting alone getting bored. As we could all afford nannies and cooks, even the housework didn't take up much of our time.

I started visiting these women in the afternoon or inviting them to my house. We drank tea together, chatted, painted each other's nails or tried out new hairdos. Sometimes one of our husbands or chauffeurs would drive us to a shopping mall. They were highly popular in Jeddah. With their huge halls they gave us the opportunity to stroll about a bit or visit a coffee shop together.

Walks outside the home weren't possible otherwise. Somewhere in the city they were always opening a new mall, and we had to check out what they had on offer because it was said to be even bigger and posher than the ones we already knew. On those occasions I tried to spend as much of Raif's money as I could on perfume, underwear and clothes. I deserved it, it seemed to me. After all, he was spending money on my rivals. Lania and I took plentiful advice at the cosmetics counter about the skin creams that were particularly in demand with Hollywood stars at the moment. "Would you like some too?" I asked my friend when I had decided to go for it.

"No, Ensaf! You're always so generous..." she half-heartedly declined. But I knew very well that I could cheer Lania up with gifts of cosmetics. So I didn't get irritated.

"I'll take two," I said to the salesgirl, and flourished Raif's credit card. "Please wrap them for us separately."

If Raif called me when I was out, I gave him short shrift. "Darling, I can't speak now. Could you call again later?" That left him quite foxed. But that was exactly what I wanted to achieve. At home I deliberately turned the music up when he rang. I wanted to let him know I had a full house — and that we were having a fantastic time without him. "Could you maybe bring pizzas for ten people when you come home?" I asked him. Raif usually agreed. Even if it went against the grain that I had a steady stream of visitors, he didn't dare protest.

Now he often came home early. If he found I wasn't there, he would call me on my mobile in a state of agitation to find out where I was. Maybe he even secretly suspected that I had tried to talk to other men as well. "I'm at my neighbor's," I would trill — delighted by his unease. "I'll be a while." Then I heard him grumbling: that it was late already, that our children might want to see their mother again before they went to bed. Such statements made me feel secretly triumphant: yes, let him be jealous, I thought to myself. After all, I was too.

It was a psychological game between me and him. A game that I could only win if I was the stronger party. I had recognized that intuitively. The more I had made myself dependent on him, the more he had turned away from me. So now I was trying to turn the tables. But it wasn't always easy to maintain the pose. Because of course I wasn't OK without him at all. In everything that I did, I was thinking of Raif.

Over time I actually became more independent. It was no longer a mere show when I met up with my friends and appeared in a good mood. There were times when I actually felt happy with them. But never completely so.

Because everything I did, I did with the goal of winning Raif back. On the one hand I was incredibly furious with him. On the other I was desperate to have him back. He was the love of my life, and my happiness depended on him.

It was a very lonely campaign, and one in which I often had to hold myself back, to keep a cool head. I fought strategically like a chess player: with weapons that hurt Raif, such as my ostentatious indifference towards him. And with weapons that were supposed to lure and seduce him. So for example I never neglected to put on nice clothes and make myself pretty for him. I went to hairdressing salons and nail studios, because I wanted him to desire me as a woman. I tried to be everything at the same time: desirable, beautiful and a little unapproachable.

And gradually, very gradually, I started to notice positive signs. It started with Raif spending more time at home. Sometimes he even brought a present back for me: a face cream, a new dress, a bouquet of flowers or something like that. I can't describe how delighted I was with these little attentions.

One thing in particular has stuck in my memory. It happened one evening, just as I was about to go to bed. Raif wasn't yet home; supposedly the work was piling up in his office. Never mind, I thought. I'd watch a bit of television. Then all of a sudden my phone rang. I saw his number. "Are you in bed already, Ensaf?" he whispered.

"As good as," I answered, surprised. Why was he asking me that?

"Are you already in your nightie?"

I was so puzzled that at first I didn't know what to say. "Yes."

"Which one?"

"The pink silk one." I knew he was especially fond of that negligee. I was pleased to register that he was breathing heavily at the other end.

"I'll send you the chauffeur, Ensaf," Raif said.

"Now?"

"Yes. Come and see me in the office."

I was quite excited when he suggested that. "Hm," I said, to keep him dangling for a while.

"But in your nightie, you hear me? Just pull your abaya over it."

"What?" I gasped for air. But I was already on fire. I had just enough time to put on the negligee that I'd already said I was wearing and sprinkle myself with Raif's favorite perfume before I pulled on the black uniform. The doorbell was already ringing. I opened the door to an extremely embarrassed Mr. Alam, who was waiting to bring me to Raif.

I got in — and pretended it was the most normal thing in the world to visit my husband at work. Raif was already waiting at the door, and he looked at me greedily. Suddenly he was my Raif again: the man I had fallen in love with, and married in the face of all kinds of resistance. So he still existed!

We had a very exciting night in his office. The next day I was on cloud nine. I felt as if Raif and I had married only yesterday. Our love had sprung back into life — and it was as if the years we had spent apart had simply blown away.

In retrospect I can shake my head over our adolescent behavior during those years. But that's how you behave when you're very young and you have no other problems in your life. And when I look back at those days I also see that the learning process I was going through at the time was very valuable. It helped to make me more independent, and thus prepared me for the life I have to lead today. A life without Raif by my side, a life alone with my children in exile.

And as for Raif: back then he was going through a profound process of internal change. Part of that included him granting me more rights as a woman.

The maturing process that Raif went through as a human being and as a man was considerably more extensive. I sensed as much. He buried himself away in his books and made new friends. People who questioned the existing social system in our country — not least in terms of its attitude to women.

That was in 2005. Five years after we met and a little more than two years after we married came a development which would change our lives forever: a bit later that same year Raif founded his Internet forum. He wanted to communicate with people who had also become thoughtful and begun to question the social order of Saudi Arabia.

# CHAPTER THREE

# LIBERAL IDEAS

Raif said nothing to me about setting up an Internet forum. That was in line with the state of our relationship at the time: he didn't think there was any need to inform me, his wife, about what he was doing and thinking. It had nothing to do with me.

I found out about it by listening in on his phone calls. At the time when our marriage wasn't going particularly well I did that regularly. And even when we came slowly closer together again, I was still very suspicious about him, and thought it safer to keep a close eye on him and his outside activities. From those scraps of conversation I learned that he often talked to his friends and acquaintances about articles published in a particular forum on the Internet. That forum had recently started playing a large part in Raif's life. Even at home he was spending more and more time at the computer, something that he had never done before. It stirred my curiosity.

One afternoon Raif left his laptop open on the dining-room table when he went to see a friend. Presumably he planned to go on working later at whatever he was doing.

I sat down at the table and touched the keyboard. The screen lit up instantly. I knew the password, because I sometimes used the computer to surf the Internet or go shopping. The browser was still open. I clicked on the history to find out what pages Raif had been navigating recently. It was always the same forum: the "network of Saudi liberals." Interested, I clicked on the address.

A field requiring a login appeared. Damn it, I didn't know Raif's access codes!

The field for the user name had already been filled in — but it wasn't clearly readable. The six black dots could be a combination of Raif's name and the year of his birth, I thought. But either way, no point worrying about it. The problem was the second, empty field.

I went to the kitchen and fetched a glass of steaming hot tea into which I stirred some sugar lumps. "Think, Ensaf!" I told myself. I tried out different words that I thought Raif might have used as a password. Najwa? Turad? Ensaf? Nothing worked. I was amazed: Raif had actually taken precautions against intervention from outside. That fired my curiosity still further.

Eventually it clicked, but in my head, not in the computer. I didn't need to crack Raif's password. Why should I use the network on his ticket? I could create an identity for myself. It was easier than I thought: I came up with an imaginary name and registered as a new user, in complete anonymity. Then I gave my own password. I now had access to the ominous site.

It was a discussion forum. I had my first big surprise on the main menu: there was my husband's full name — as founder and publisher of the website. He and a doctor friend had set up the site together. I was dumbfounded: what was

Raif doing behind my back? And above all, why was he doing it secretly? Why didn't he involve me?

I carefully read the articles. They were all about similar subjects: the social situation in Saudi Arabia, religion, human rights, and explicitly women's rights. There were a particularly large number of articles on that subject, in fact. All the articles were avidly discussed by the members of the network. And for each of them Raif had written a short commentary and replied to the author.

People should be assessed according to moral, not religious standards, I read in the articles that he particularly praised. I was astonished. Because until recently Raif had been quite fastidious about keeping religious rules. After Najwa was born he went through a phase during which he often listened to cassettes of religious advice, kept meticulously to prayer times and fasted strictly at Ramadan. It was the period after the attacks on September 11, 2001, when many Saudis adopted an even stricter reading of Islam. And Raif too had tended in that direction.

What surprised me particularly, however, was how committed and critical he was in his statements about the social position of women in Saudi Arabia: they must no longer be treated as second-class citizens, and should at last have more rights, he wrote, demanding women's right to vote. What on earth, I thought irritably. Were those really Raif's words? What was he writing there? And what was he trying to achieve?

I can't say that what I read made me particularly happy or even filled me with pride — what I felt was concern. It was plain from the outset that Raif's remarks would cause trouble. They used the exact tone that always gave our religious police an allergic reaction. And the religious police are extraordinarily powerful. Anyone picking a fight with them is playing with fire.

And the blog also made me furious with Raif: everything he wrote sounded wonderful. Where the content was concerned, I agreed with him a hundred percent. But I couldn't help comparing his words with his behavior. What hypocrisy! There's this guy making public pronouncements about women's rights, while at home he's behaving like every other Saudi macho man.

Irritated and confused, I snapped the computer shut. I didn't say a word to Raif about the fact that I had looked at his website. A wife, I said to myself, must be able to keep a few secrets from her husband. After all, I hadn't told Raif anything about the Facebook and Twitter accounts that I ran under a pseudonym. I wanted to keep myself in the picture, while playing my cards close to my chest.

From now on I industriously read everything he wrote. And I challenged him, by demanding that he put his theoretical statements into practice. In the blog Raif often discussed the subject of the segregation of the sexes, which is practiced to an extreme in Saudi Arabia. In his articles he criticized the strict segregation of men and women, and pointed out that it was not due to a religious commandment, but was a fashion from the past few decades.

When I'd read something like that, I put him to the test. "I think we should invite more people to our house," I said. "How about you bring your friends home more often?"

"But you have lots of friends," he replied irritably.

"Yes, but I would like to meet *your* friends too."

"Hm…" he said and thought for a moment. "Maybe I'll

ask Mohammed if he wants to bring his wife along. Then you could talk to each other." Mohammed had become, I knew, a good acquaintance of Raif's.

"Yes, but I want to meet them both," I insisted. "Mohammed too. I'd like to join in when you talk to each other."

"Hm," Raif repeated, and frowned. At first he had real difficulty transferring his noble demands to private and everyday life. One's "own" wife was something quite different from women in general. It was easy to demand a few rights for other women. But applying them to your own family required from him a much more fundamental reorientation, and a profound interrogation of his own values.

But Raif did actually change over time. I think he eventually understood that what he wrote was not echoing unheard in a vacuum, but reached me in some form or other. His words cried out for consequences in real life. And Raif faced that challenge — as a man, and as a husband: he struggled hard with himself to harmonize the abstract liberal ideas with his real feelings.

It was mostly reading that helped with that. Inspired by the stimulation of other authors on the network, he started reading more than before.

At first he was interested in early Islamic thinkers, some of whom had fallen into oblivion, and historical works. He engaged intensely with the history of our region, as well as with the more recent history of Europe. He was particularly drawn to the French Revolution. The Enlightenment thinkers fascinated him, and he read everything about secularism and liberalism. But apart from the European theorists, in his engagement with these concepts he was influenced by Arab intellectuals like the Syrian Farah Antun, who had traced the backwardness of the Arab world to the strictness of its faith. Or Abdullah al-Qasemi, an intellectual very controversial in the Arab world who, in his late work, radically advocated a separation of state and religion and even doubted the existence of God.

I myself, I must admit, avoided this kind of reading. I glanced once or twice at the books on Raif's bedside table, but usually gave up after a few paragraphs: the complicated thoughts described in them, and the abstract formulations, tired me very quickly.

But I'm pretty sure that it was mostly these books that changed Raif in the end, and did so fundamentally. First Raif changed his ideas — and then his behavior toward me, his wife. His demands stopped being mere theory. They became a serious matter for him, which he began to live with every fiber of his being.

His transformation was apparent in many different ways. The most conspicuous for me was that Raif became more domestic. He no longer worked around the clock, but spent much more time with me and the children.

Raif had always been crazy about his children. But now he tried to play an active part in their upbringing. It almost made me laugh when he tried to change Dodi's nappy for the first time and asked me how it actually worked. I patiently explained to him how you cleaned the little one, got rid of the old nappy and fastened the new one in place. He didn't turn a hair. He roller-skated in the sitting room with Najwa, by now a delightful three-year-old, and organized extended pillow fights.

Soon I fell pregnant again; to be quite honest it was an

accident. Two children would have been enough for me. But Raif was deliriously happy and was touchingly concerned about me, almost as he had been the first time. In the evening he often "cooked" for us, by bringing fast food home. Or else he would invite his friends to our house so that I could meet them. He would never have done that before, even under threat of punishment.

They were an illustrious circle of journalists, writers, artists, but also people with power and influence. As almost all of them still live in Saudi Arabia — and the spin put on their friendship with us wasn't necessarily seen in a very positive light in our country — I won't mention any names.

The most important thing for me was that Raif had stopped leaving me alone as often as before. That was what had hurt me the most. Now, if he was still busy in the evening he sometimes brought his work home and sat down with his laptop at our dining-room table. When he wanted to write another article for his forum, for example. That meant that I got a clearer idea of what he was currently working on. Sometimes he even asked me my opinion on a particular subject or an idea for a piece.

"Write something about the relationships between women and other women," I once suggested.

He looked at me quizzically. "What do you mean?"

"Well, you know." I fidgeted on my chair. "When women exchange caresses. When they kiss and so on."

"They do that?"

Raif listened in horror. He clearly had no idea what was going on sexually in the parallel world of women. In fact the phenomenon of lesbian love is relatively widespread in our country.

"Yes, of course," I said. "I know a lot of women who don't like their husbands — or are neglected by them. And then..."

"Then what?"

"Then they just look for a substitute." I explained to him that it is much too risky for women to take a male lover. Because for a Saudi woman that would mean putting her whole existence, her life on the line. If she is caught in adultery, she is rejected — in the worst case, even stoned. So women prefer to fulfill their desire for love, intimacy and tenderness mutually. There are many advantages to that: women are more accessible to women. And if they are actually caught exchanging cuddles, it isn't immediately seen as sex. And since the phenomenon does not officially exist, the Damocles sword of adultery does not hang over it.

"I didn't know anything about that," Raif admitted. He looked at me suspiciously — as if he was desperate to ask me, "I don't suppose you ever...?" But he didn't go on with his question. And I just laughed. I liked to leave him in a state of uncertainty. In the end Raif said I was right: it was an excellent subject, since no one had ever written about it before. And he immediately sat down to write an article on the forum about it.

All of these changes showed me that Raif was really serious: he wanted free of his old life and his old-fashioned habits. He even thought about selling the institute. I liked the idea very much — and I backed him up in it: it meant that he would get away from the many women he dealt with daily. He would finally close this chapter.

But of course the change didn't happen from one day to the next. First of all we needed a buyer and a good offer. And that was going to turn out to be a difficult undertaking. If the authorities had already given Raif a hard time because he had a reputation, now they really had him in their sights — but no longer because of his former adventures. Those were passé. Now they had it in for him because Raif's forum was arousing their suspicion. They now used any alleged shortcomings at the institute as an excuse to make life hard for him.

It was a while before we understood who he was actually up against: the religious police. After Raif had set up his website, they had more or less torn his "case" out of the hands of the education authorities.

The religious police is the organization of clerics and ultraconservatives. Their main function is to boss the population around and impose on them the extremely strict codes of behavior of Wahhabism. There are historical reasons why such an institution exists: you have to know that the state of Saudi Arabia grew out of an alliance between the Islamic religious scholar Mohammed Ibn Abd al-Wahhab and the al-Saud family. This alliance was concluded in the lifetime of Abd al-Wahhab, almost 300 years ago — but in essence it continues until the present day.

According to tradition, Abd al-Wahhab gave the then head of the al-Saud family, Muhammad Ibn al-Saud, religious legitimacy for his claim to power. In return, the al-Sauds supported the spread of Abd al-Wahhab's teachings, later known after him as the "Wahhabiya." Today it is our state ideology — and at the same time the ideology followed by all terrorists from al-Qaeda to Islamic State. Because all of those movements have their ideological origin in our country.

As one might imagine, Abd al-Wahhab represented a very extreme version of Islam. He thought the holy scriptures gave a detailed depiction of community life in the early Islamic communities of Mecca and Medina. He had a highly idealized view of those communities; he saw them as containing the purity of the divine teaching. He accused the believers of his time of moving away from that ideal state — and thus demanded a return to the literal imposition of God's laws. It goes without saying that he thought he knew better than all of his colleagues.

This radical preacher rejected all the innovations that the Islamic religion had made in the course of the centuries. That referred above all to Muslim saints: the worship of the saints contradicted the core essence, the absolute monotheism, of Islam, he preached — and during his life, in the eighteenth century, he destroyed the domes, mosques and graves of companions of the Prophet. Later Wahhabists even destroyed Mohammed's birthplace in Mecca, which was revered as a place of pilgrimage. Today extremists all over the world refer to these arguments when they wipe out the remains of ancient cultures. Islamic State destroying ancient statues in Nineveh in Iraq. Al-Qaeda in the Maghreb destroying all the Sufi shrines in the desert city of Timbuktu. And the Afghan Taliban blowing up the big Buddha statues of Bamiyan.

But Abd al-Wahhab also fought against everyday objects, claiming that they had no place in original Islamic society: tobacco-smoking, listening to music, dance and song, the wearing of clothing made of silk. According to his militantly purist teachings, all of these things keep people away from faith.

In Saudi society many of these abstruse rules remain valid today: our cemeteries, for example, are completely unadorned — a late consequence of Abd al-Wahhab's conclusion that all funeral monuments that serve to honor the dead are to be considered idolatrous and should therefore be removed. Because of him there are no cinemas, no public concerts, no dances or discos. And with every technological innovation — such as the introduction of the radio or later of television — Wahhabi clerics sense the decline of the East. The strict rules concerning women's clothing also date back to the laws that Abd al-Wahhab derived from the Qur'an and the Sunnah.

How can a preacher who has been dead for over 200 years still have such influence? The answer is simple: it was made possible by his continued alliance with the temporal power. Or perhaps we should talk about a symbiosis between the clergy and the ruling house of al-Saud? The alliance was tenable because both parties knew each other and could only enlarge their field of influence together. The pious Abd al-Wahhab preached that all non-Wahhabi Muslims had to be fought in the jihad, the holy religious war. By doing that, he provided the ideological basis for the expansion of the state of the al-Saud family, who gradually conquered almost all of the Arab peninsula.

It is the descendants of these historic allies who rule the state even today. The al-Sauds are in charge of the economy and politics. The descendants of Abd al-Wahhab — they are also known as Al ash-Shaikh, the family of the sheikh — control religious life, education and to some extent justice.

Every time our monarchs need the support of the sheikh, in the form of a fatwa, for example, a legal opinion, the influence of the imams, the senior religious clergy, is particularly strong. That is why no one dares to defy their executive organization, the religious police. The force is a kind of state within a state, and leads an uncontrolled life of its own. Sometimes it even arrests citizens who have not infringed any state law. Women wearing heels that are too high, or too much perfume. It is simply accepted. No one intervenes in such cases, because no one wants to pick a fight with the mighty religious establishment.

And that was exactly what my Raif was doing now. He completely ignored the limits on thinking that the clerics dictated to the population. I'm not sure how naive he was being — or how aware he was of the risk. Perhaps a bit of both. At any rate he had a real desire to write what he really thought. A desire that was much stronger than any possible misgivings.

I could tell that things were getting more serious by the fact that Raif now ran the forum mostly from his private laptop. I had known for ages about the problems he was dealing with at the institute and the constant inspections that were carried out there. If Raif generally didn't tell me anything about it, I had my own sources. But while in the old days shortcomings at the institute had been the object of such investigations, Raif as a person was now the focus of police interest: several times the inspectors turned his office upside down and copied all the data on his computer. Raif put on a relaxed face, but his unease was mounting and could no longer be hidden.

There is no law in Saudi Arabia forbidding anyone from operating a website. To that extent Raif wasn't doing anything illegal. I even think the royal house knew his site — and tolerated it, so that their subjects could let off a little steam there. Certainly, there were royal spies among the registered users and they read everything that was written there. As long as no one criticized the monarch himself, at the time everything was fine as far as our temporal rulers were concerned.

To the religious side of state power it looked quite different, however: for them the line had been crossed long ago. The omnipotence of the imams was generally viewed critically on the site — or, even worse, the participants in the forum made fun of it. Since the religious police had nothing on Raif at first, they were eagerly looking for evidence to bring a trial against him. But they couldn't find anything. So they took the easier path and tried to take the website off the Net. But to their great annoyance they discovered that for technical reasons they couldn't just delete the forum. Of course the site was run by a foreign server. So they decided to resort to more extreme methods.

One evening Raif came home white as a sheet and immediately wanted to go to bed. I asked him what was up. "I was at the police station today; they questioned me for several hours," he reported despondently.

He stared at his laptop, which sat as always on the dining-room table. Then he looked at my fat belly. By now I was heavily pregnant and would soon bring our third child into the world. Najwa and Dodi were playing noisily in the living room. Raif ran his hand over my bump and smiled sadly. I think that at that moment he realized that he wasn't the only one who would have to pay a price for his activities: his family would too. He didn't want to bring his problems home, but there was no getting around it.

Some weeks later, shortly after my third child, who we called Miriam, was born at the end of 2007, the police came to the house for the first time. There was a ring on the doorbell at about half past nine. I was still in bed — and wondered who was paying us a visit so early in the morning. One of our women neighbors, perhaps? Raif opened the door. There were four police officers there, three men and one woman. None of them wore a uniform. The woman — like all Saudi women — was swathed in black fabric from head to toe. She held her police badge under his nose and demanded to be allowed entry.

"Of course, come in," I heard him saying, "I'll just tell my wife. Please have a seat in the meantime."

A short time later Raif was standing in my bedroom doorway. He looked rather embarrassed. "We have a visit from the police, darling," he said. "But don't let that worry you. Just stay here in the room and rest."

Naturally I was anything but thrilled by this "visit." I hastily crawled out of bed and swapped my pajamas for jeans and a T-shirt. I was still very sleepy and a little unsteady on my feet, as I had only come out of the hospital a few days before. Miriam, who had just been feeding at my breast, was asleep in her crib. I don't think it unlikely that the police chose the date, so soon after her birth, to show us our vulnerability as a family. And they did it splendidly.

I listened frozen as our apartment was turned upside down on the other side of my door. Oh dear, I thought: I hoped that Raif had a good explanation ready for Najwa and Dodi, so that they weren't too terrified. As I later discovered, the police didn't stop at the nursery door. They were looking for reading matter. Forbidden reading matter: as in Nazi Germany, there were — and still are — books in the kingdom that are on the index. Among them are the works of many famous authors, such as Iraq's well-known poets Badr Shaker al-Sayyab and Abdul Wahhab al-Bayati, or the Palestinian poets Muin Bseiso and Mahmoud Darwish. Raif thought very highly of their writings.

A short time later there was a knock at my door. "Yes, who is it?" I called.

The policewoman came in. "Good morning, madame," she said. "I would like to ask you a few questions."

"Of course," I replied in as friendly a voice as I could manage. In fact my heart was about to burst. What did this black crow think she was doing? Why was she snuffling around in our house? Who or what gave her the right?

She asked me my name, the number of children I had, many things that struck me as entirely irrelevant. Whether our house was bought or rented. Whether the institute belonged to Raif alone, or whether there were other partners. What time he normally came home in the evening. And whether he talked to me about his Internet forum and his ideas. "No, not at all. I'm not interested in it," I replied.

Last of all she wanted to know what books Raif had been reading lately. "My husband doesn't tell me things like that," I told her.

She didn't seem convinced. "Have you any books here in the room?" she asked, looking me severely in the eyes through the eye-slit of her niqab.

"Not that I'm aware."

"If you'll allow me, I would like to check for myself."

"Go ahead!" With a gesture I let her know that she could feel free to look around.

She had no inhibitions: she looked under the bed, opened the wardrobe and inspected the drawers of both of our bedside tables. Last of all she lifted the mattress. The whole thing reminded me a little of my brothers' searches in the old days. Miriam, who sensed the unease in the room, started crying.

The policewoman took a step toward the crib. For a

moment I thought she was actually going to look under the newborn baby's blanket. But then she probably thought better of it.

"What a sweet little thing," she said. "Let's leave it for the time being." To me that sounded half conciliatory, half threatening. What did she mean "for the time being"?

The police officers took away almost all our books, Raif's computer and all the data storage devices we had in the flat. Both our little ones watched them uncomprehendingly as they left. "Who were they, Dad?" asked Najwa, who at the age of four could already tell that this had not been a normal visit.

"They were very curious people," said Raif. "I'm sure they won't come back."

Raif himself believed his own promise least of all: after what had happened he was very worried. When the police invaded our flat, they had scared him senseless, just as they had planned. But Raif tried to keep it secret from me. He glossed over his insecurity so as not to frighten me. That's typical behavior in our cultural circle—and it's not meant badly, but considerately. Still, I would rather he had shared his concerns with me. The worse the harassment from the police, the less I learned about it from Raif.

By now we jumped every time the doorbell rang. Once I was there when they took him away from the flat. There was nothing left of the forced politeness of their first visit. Two men, both in plain clothes, forced their way into our flat, told Raif to turn around, blindfolded him and took him somewhere secret for questioning. When Raif came back, his whole body was covered with bruises and welts, and he didn't say a word for several days, either to me or to his friends.

Another time he called me from the station and told me he wasn't sure if they were going to let him go again. I sat at home for a terrified twenty-four hours and waited for news. But there was no sign of Raif. His phone was switched off. In my despair I phoned his friend Turad. But even he didn't know what was going on.

When Raif reappeared the next day, pale and exhausted, he played the story down: the police had only wanted to intimidate him. In fact they had nothing on him.

I knew that Raif was basically right: all of these measures only served to erect a threatening façade. The police wanted to show him how vulnerable he was, and give him the feeling that they could do what they wanted to him. Again and again they demanded that he take down the website. But Raif stubbornly refused. "The forum isn't breaking any law," he argued. "It's just a way for people to exchange ideas."

A few months later a car suddenly appeared in front of our house: a silver Mitsubishi Lancer. Raif noticed it first. "That car looks weird to me," he said, moving the kitchen curtain aside a little to get a better view. "It's always down there."

I shrugged. "Perhaps one of the neighbors has a new car?"

"So why doesn't he park it down there, in the underground car park?"

"Hm." I went over to him and tried to get a better look at the car as well. I had to crane my neck slightly. I even put my glasses on. Was there someone sitting in it? Hard to say. You could hardly see inside through the dark car windows.

"There's something odd about it," Raif admitted.

"What do you mean?"

"I don't know. Someone might be watching us."

I couldn't get his suspicion out of my head. From now on, whenever I had a free moment I looked at the car. It was spooky. It never moved from the spot. I never saw anyone getting in or out. As if someone had parked the car there and forgotten about it.

A few days later Raif came home with Turad late in the evening. Because it was so late I wasn't exactly delighted with him for bringing a visitor with him. But I immediately hurried to the kitchen to fetch them tea and cakes. "Forget that," Raif said when I came into the sitting room with the tray. "You need to pack your things."

I looked at him, dumbfounded. "Do you know what time it is? The children are already asleep."

"Get on with it," Raif urged. "We haven't much time."

As I clearly wasn't being quick enough, he himself went into the bedroom and stuffed some clothes for us in a traveling bag. "What's going on?" I asked, watching him. But Raif didn't give me an explanation. He packed a few things for Najwa and Dodi as well, then woke the children.

"We're going on a little outing," he said cheerfully. They sleepily rubbed their eyes.

"To Grandma's?" asked Najwa, remembering that we had visited my parents in Jizan shortly after Miriam was born. But Raif hadn't come with us.

"No," he replied, "to a place you've never been before."

That didn't sound good to me. "I don't suppose you'd let me know what you're actually planning?" I hissed.

"Have you got everything?" he asked, rather than answering. He took my abaya from the hook and gave it to me. "Put that on." When I was wrapped up, he laid the baby in my arms. Then he pushed us toward the door. Turad carried our bags. We took the lift down to the underground car park. There we got into Turad's car, while Raif's car stayed where it was.

"What's this all about?" I protested as we drove out of the garage. Although it was slowly dawning on me that we were giving the driver of the Mitsubishi the runaround: Raif didn't want them to notice us disappearing from the flat. "You can't just leave spontaneously with three children," I went on, nonetheless. "Why are we leaving in the middle of the night?"

I think Raif was quite annoyed with me at this point. At any rate, he didn't say anything more. But Turad, who was always very polite toward me, played the gentleman. "Your husband has your best interests at heart, madame," he said, defending Raif. "Believe me, it's all for your own protection." Yes, yes, I even believed him when he said that. But I was still furious because Raif had fallen back into his old ways, and had made all the decisions over my head.

He brought us to a small flat furnished with nothing but a sofa. I think the flat belonged to Turad. There wasn't even a carpet, a microwave or a television. "I hope you're not expecting us to live here?" I said to Raif.

"It's only for a short time," he reassured me. "Just till I know what that guy is up to."

"What am I supposed to do here all day with the children?"

I thought the little flat was awful. There was absolutely nothing to do there. Najwa and Dodi whined all the time because they were so bored. And then Miriam started wailing as well. It was too much to bear.

After two or three days Turad came with news: he had talked to the porter at our old house. He reported that the guy in the car had asked about us after we vanished from his radar so suddenly. He had been at his wits' end. Raif had taken that as proof. "You see now that I was right?" he said to me. "The guy was employed to keep us under surveillance."

"Fine," I said, "so what does that mean now? We can't stay here, at any rate." It may sound funny. Particularly from our present point of view, now that I know all Raif's fears were justified. But while I was in the situation itself it felt different: practical matters, not least my own comfort, were more important to me than strategic considerations. That was why I urged Raif to go back to our flat. I just wanted to go on living my normal life. I repressed everything else as best I could.

"OK. But only until I've found something new," he said at last, giving in to my gripes.

So we went back home. The Mitsubishi was still there. Now the man shadowing us barely attempted to hide what he was up to: he brazenly got in and out of the car, and even smoked the occasional cigarette when the time dragged.

Meanwhile Raif went flat-hunting with Turad. He texted me pictures of the places they viewed together. I rejected lots of them because they looked too small, or because they were in an area that I didn't like. As I didn't want to lose my friends, I had asked him not to move too far away. In the end Raif found a big, beautiful flat only a few streets away from our old one. I was contented, and declared myself in agreement.

At dead of night the porter from the institute and some

other assistants helped us to move our furniture from the old flat to the new one. Mitsubishi man didn't get wind of this, because he wasn't in his place that night. He sometimes disappeared for a while. It was a weight off Raif's mind when we finally stopped having to worry about him. And to be honest it was a weight off mine too.

I devoted a lot of energy to furnishing our new abode. I enjoyed looking for furniture and ordering it on the Internet. As Raif isn't particularly good at DIY I paid for it to be assembled as well — and put everything on his credit card. In this way it was soon cozy in our new home.

But the problems didn't stop. The fact that we had shaken off the man who was tailing us didn't mean that the police would leave Raif in peace: they regularly summoned him and questioned him about the latest articles on his website, about which they were fully informed.

As operator of the forum Raif was responsible for all statements made on it, they warned him. That seriously worried Raif. Because it left the gateway wide open for his enemies: if someone involved in one of the discussions insulted the king — a capital crime in Saudi Arabia — he, Raif, would be held responsible. We had no idea whether that was legal or illegal. At any rate it put Raif's fate completely in the hands of those who had crept surreptitiously in to the user group, purely in order to bring the forum into disrepute.

Raif was regularly exhausted when he came home from being questioned. Afterward he wouldn't go to his office for days at a time. "It can't go on like this," I said to him when he lay half-dead on the sofa yet again after a night at the station. "You need to relax and get away from it all."

"That's a good idea," Raif said. "How about we go away with the children?"

I thought his suggestion was great. Raif paused for a moment. "Maybe that's the solution anyway," he said thoughtfully.

"What do you mean?"

"I could run the site from abroad."

"You want to leave Saudi Arabia?" I was very surprised by his idea. It was the first time Raif had said anything like this. He had never mentioned the idea of turning his back on his homeland. He wanted to change it, after all.

"We could at least take a look at what possibilities there are."

I agreed. Raif got us tickets to Malaysia. And a few days later the whole family was sitting on a plane to Kuala Lumpur.

We had a wonderful time there. We would never be as close again as a family as we were in those four weeks. We spent most of our time in a hotel on the beach, where I could sunbathe while Raif built sand castles or played in the water with the children. He spoiled us to the hilt — and each of us in different ways. Najwa got the Barbie doll of her dreams. He flattered me with a new black and orange swimming costume with daring slits up the sides that revealed my skin. He let the warm waves wash around our baby Miriam, nine months old at the time, until she gurgled with pleasure. And with Dodi he took an outing to the island of Langkawi where he bought the boy so much ice cream that he was sick.

Crashing into the midst of that idyll was some news that I thought was the best in the world: Turad had found a buyer for the institute! He and Raif had received a good offer at last.

And as they were both fed up with having problems with the authorities, they wanted to go for it. "Do you agree that we should sell the thing?" he asked me, not least because he needed my signature on the paper. Officially I was a partner because of my teaching diploma.

"Nothing I'd like more," I replied wholeheartedly. I'd wished the damn thing would go to hell for ages! So yes, get rid of it.

We printed the contract in a public Internet shop. Raif and I signed together. When we had scanned in the document and Raif clicked "send" on his email, I felt a great burden lifting from me. We were free! Raif no longer had any professional obligations in Saudi Arabia. We could really stay in Malaysia if we wanted to.

Raif investigated under what conditions foreigners could acquire capital in the country and establish companies or become partners in them. And how to apply for a long-term residence permit. He particularly liked the idea of running his forum from here in future because it meant he knew our family was safe. The idea was not unusual: there were many mavericks who had moved abroad to find peace from the Saudi authorities.

I wouldn't have minded staying in Malaysia with its warm, humid climate, spanking clean cities and friendly Asians: I really liked it all. I could easily have imagined bringing up my three children in this environment. Perhaps in a smart apartment with a swimming pool where I would enjoy the sun while next to me Raif wrote his articles over a drink. That was my idealized vision of the future.

What's that thing they say? If you want to make God laugh, tell him your dreams! It wasn't so simple by any means.

The foreign language turned out to be a greater obstacle than we had thought: with English alone, which neither we nor the Malays spoke particularly well, you wouldn't get far in the working environment. We also established that we knew too little about this beautiful country to open a business here and derive a reliable income from it. The culture, the people, the language: it was all very nice, but still a complete mystery to us. And we couldn't take big risks with our capital, because we had three children to care for.

There was also the fact that more and more friends were calling Raif on his phone to find out where he had been for so long. His political companions urged him to come back to Saudi Arabia, or at least to the Middle East. They promised they would be there for him if the police harassment didn't stop.

"They're all urging me to come back soon," he said to me. "And I don't know whether emigration is the right way to go."

"Do you want us to go home?" I asked him.

"Of course I'd like to be there," he admitted to me. "I need to talk to people. I need to know what moves them. Here, a long way away, I'm really cut off. How can I fight for social transformation from here?"

"Then we have to go home," I said, because I knew how important these things were for Raif.

But even that made him unhappy. He was totally torn within himself. "Is that really what you want, Ensaf?" he asked me. "We'll never be at ease there. At least not as long as the website exists. The police are just waiting to hold me responsible for everything that's been discussed there while we've been away."

"They have no right!"

"Right? Since when has that been the issue? The police are just looking for a scapegoat." He tore his hair. "I really don't know whether I can inflict that on you and the children. I want the five of us to be able to lead a normal, peaceful life. A life without fear. You understand?"

I nodded. "Yes, that's what I would like too."

In the end we agreed to postpone Project Emigration. We couldn't run away, we thought — and we were wrong. But who could have guessed that we would never again have the chance to leave the country together?

Just a few days after our return, reality caught up with us. The police summoned Raif for a long interrogation. I don't know exactly what they threatened him with. It must have been pretty serious. They also took his computer away.

He looked half-dead when he came home. "What do you think, Ensaf?" he asked me. "Should I give up the website?"

I was amazed that he wanted to hear my advice. So I thought for a long time before I answered him. On the one hand I knew how important Raif's forum was to him. On the other hand it was clear to me that the pressure that was now starting up again was likely to finish him off.

"Give it up for a while," I suggested. "Maybe then you'll have a bit of peace again. Or we'll find another solution."

He nodded sadly. "You're right, Ensaf," he said. "You're very clever. Don't let anyone tell you otherwise."

"Not even you?" I asked with a wink.

He knew exactly what I was referring to. "Especially not me. You know, we men always think we have to have the last word. Please don't be cross with me if I've sometimes under-estimated you."

I kissed him passionately. I don't think any Saudi man

apart from him has ever confessed such a thing to his wife. During the years of our marriage Raif had undergone an impressive evolution.

He actually took my advice—and in 2009 he took the website down.

# CHAPTER FOUR

# "INCORRECTLY FORMATTED"

Once the institute had been sold and the forum closed down, we had to reorganize our lives on every level. First of all there was the question of how we were going to earn a living from now on. Raif is pretty inventive in these matters: he has a good sense of how things work, and can spot gaps in the market.

One big problem in Saudi Arabia is unemployment, particularly among young people. At the beginning I mentioned that I registered with a state office after completing my studies, with a view to being offered a job at some point. It's what people do. But in reality no one expects to find anything. There's simply far too little work. Jobs for women are particularly thin on the ground: my sister Egbal, for example, waited ten years for her first offer. And after registering I never heard from the office again.

In other words, it was pointless. And women who needed to earn money—for example because their husband had thrown them out, or, in the case of my sister, had died, had a real problem. A problem that Raif now wanted to solve:

together with Turad, he founded in Jeddah the first employment agency for women.

I can't claim to have been particularly thrilled by the
idea. I thought it was good — and I also thought that it might
work. But when I realized that he would be dealing only with
women again, my old suspicion welled up in me. Admittedly
Raif had changed. But he was an attractive man. Would he be
able to resist temptation?

I tried to suppress my unease. It wasn't fair of me to suspect Raif in anticipation. After all, he was my husband — and
he had to earn money for our family. That was his duty; I
couldn't really stick my oar in. So I fought an internal battle
and finally forced myself to let him have his way: if our family
was to work, I had to learn to trust him completely again.

It was the right decision. Because as I was soon able to
convince myself, Raif really was no longer interested in
flirting with the women he was professionally involved with.
Although I'm sure plenty of them would have willingly gone
along with it. His attitude had changed fundamentally: he
no longer saw the women who came to his agency as sexual
objects — as most Saudi men would have done. He saw them
as human beings, to be taken seriously and respected.

He really wanted to help these women, many of whom
had fallen into a state of distress: "Women need work just as
urgently as men do, in fact sometimes even more so!" he said,
defending them in an article for the newspaper *Al-Bilal*. "So
will we finally stop our unjust and patriarchal chitter-chatter?
Or do we want to keep on waging war on Saudi women who
need to earn their living?"

Raif gave his views on the subject in a number of newspaper articles. He had worked out that women in our society

are treated as second-class citizens, which fundamentally contradicted his humanist conviction that all human beings are equal and should therefore have the same rights. So now he put all his passion into demanding more rights for them. With his committed articles on the forum he had made a name for himself among newspaper editors as a liberal thinker and human rights activist, and got a lot of requests to write columns and opinion pieces as a result.

But he couldn't forget his own discussion forum. Raif had never planned to allow it to disappear completely. The platform had been an important part of his life — and precisely what Saudi civil society most urgently needed, in his view: a space where citizens, men and women, could express their opinions and discuss them together.

"We need to talk to each other a lot more and agree on the standards by which we want to live in this country," he said to me one evening over dinner. Then I knew: it was only a matter of time before the site was back on the Net. I didn't contradict him. Raif needed that forum — and Saudi Arabia needed it too. What right did I have to oppose it? The site was in his DNA; it was his calling.

I didn't have to wait very long for my prophecy to come true: in early 2010 Raif set up a new Internet forum with the women's rights activist Souad al-Shammari. He chose a name that was almost identical to that of the earlier site. The "Network of Saudi Liberals" became the "Saudi Liberal Network." In translation the small difference becomes almost nonexistent.

This time, unlike before, I played a very active part in setting up the website. It was Raif himself who persuaded me: he told me all the details of the preparations that he had made for the site, and the changes he had considered. As he wanted to reach a wider public, this time the texts were also to be accessible to non-registered members. The secret service would read it anyway, he argued. I thought that was interesting but also dangerous. Raif was sure to create even more of a scandal by doing it that way.

The day the site went up on the Net, the whole family went on an outing to el-Sherah, a leisure park with a pretty garden and various swimming pools for the children. It is on a spit of land in Jeddah, and surrounded by the sea on all sides. A very pleasant place. Raif took us to a fish restaurant there for lunch.

His laptop was on his lap, and he watched with excitement what was happening on the website, which had only been up for a few minutes. His liberal friends all knew that he was planning a new start, and they had all given it word-of-mouth publicity. That was why so many visitors turned up immediately, eager to read Raif's opening blog and comment on it. But to do that they first had to register: under either a pseudonym or their real name, as they wished.

With every new registration Raif shouted out with jubilation. "We've got twenty users now," he cried, "Now it's twenty-one!" He was as excited as if it was an auction where the important thing was to get the highest possible price. And I was excited too.

The new network quickly gained fame and popularity. More and more users registered to join in with the discussion. After only a week there were already several thousand. Raif was very happy that such a high number had joined, and I suspected that he was secretly bursting with pride.

It was only now the forum existed again that I realized just how much he had missed the exchange with other liberal thinkers over the past few months. He was really addicted to it. He sat day and night at his laptop, writing articles, reading everything that was written and adding his comments. Raif was the hope and brain of the forum. He kept it alive with his ideas, and at the same time the forum kept him alive. It released an incredible energy and productivity in him.

For me it was a real joy to see him so vital and euphoric. So full of energy for what was, without a doubt, his vocation.

One evening, after he had once again spent the whole day on his beloved forum, I set down a box of takeaway pizza beside his laptop. Without taking his eye off the screen, he reached out for a piece of diavolo. "Ensaf, you're really impossible," he complained.

"How come?"

"You don't support your husband!"

At first I thought he was commenting on his dinner. "Would you like something else? There's some leftover rice and vegetables in the fridge."

But Raif was already wolfing down his pizza — and reading, apparently immersed in it, some article or other. "I don't mean in terms of food," he said, correcting me, "I mean here in the forum!" At last he looked up to me. He grinned at me cheekily with his beautiful eyes. "Do you think it's actually OK that everyone is registering for the forum, and you — my own wife — aren't one of them?"

Now I couldn't help laughing. "Oh, Raif," I said condescendingly. "Do you really think I would do that to you? Of course I registered ages ago!"

"You did what?"

"I was one of the first," I admitted, smiling victoriously. "We've even communicated with each other."

Raif gasped. I'd left him completely flummoxed. "What's your user name?" he asked me at last.

I sat down on his lap and drew the laptop on the table toward me. Raif didn't stop me. My fingers darted over the keys until my user profile appeared on the screen, with a list of all the traces I had left on the forum: I had commented on a number of articles. And of course I was particularly proud of the comments that Raif had ennobled with his agreement, unaware that I had written them under a pseudonym.

He couldn't believe it. "All this stuff that you're doing behind my back!" he said, apparently furious. But in his words I could clearly hear the admiration that my secret deeds inspired in him. "I wouldn't have thought you capable of it," he said, a bit too honestly for my liking.

Raif urged me to come out from behind my pseudonym. He showed me articles by a few famous journalists and writers who also used their real names in the forum. "Look, more and more people are writing under their real names," he said. "It's time to come clean: as the editor's wife you should do that too. What century are we living in?"

This was before the Arab Spring—and a liberal breeze was blowing through Saudi Arabia. More and more people were daring to come out from hiding. It was a positive development.

But I liked the idea for quite a different reason. I had registered under a pseudonym and told Raif nothing about it partly because I wasn't sure if he would be happy about my activity on the forum. Would he be happy that I, his wife, was invading his world? And on the other hand, where the content was concerned: wasn't there a chance of him finding what I had to say ridiculous?

My self-confidence was rather weak in this respect. I knew that Raif was a very elegant writer: he can formulate his ideas so smoothly that everyone applauds him for it. Unfortunately I don't have that talent. Or at least I've never been able to develop it. So I was entering uncertain territory. For precisely that reason I had been incredibly glad when Raif reacted positively to one of my comments: so we were thinking along similar lines.

And now he was going one better: I saw his challenge as a new compliment to the quality of my remarks. Because if he had found them embarrassing, he would hardly have wanted to show the whole world that they came from his wife. But Raif was genuinely proud of me, and even encouraged me to come further to the fore. In the end he was the one who turned my pseudonym into my actual name, while I looked over his shoulder. Now we appeared as a couple in his forum. It gave our relationship a whole new quality.

From that moment I appeared on the network like a completely normal, fully fledged member of the discussion group. Of course I didn't write nearly as much as Raif. My children didn't let me: whenever they saw me sitting at the computer, they demanded that I play with them instead. And in fact Raif too preferred it when I paid attention to him rather than the screen. When they were all asleep in the evening, meanwhile, I was often too tired. Then I would watch a bit of television rather than setting my wits to work.

But there were subjects that made my blood boil. Above all the subject of women. That was why I wrote about it on the forum: mostly I described events from my everyday life, which clearly demonstrated the systematic discrimination promoted by our government. And once I even risked a piece of generalized criticism: I lamented the rules on veil-wearing, the ban on driving, the unfair inheritance law and the medieval guardianship system in Saudi Arabia. All the things that made my life as a woman difficult. Later this article would be published in the newspaper *El Hayat* — and Raif was bursting with pride. "Ensaf, my Ensaf," he said fondly. "You're really far more on the ball than I would have thought possible!"

I clapped him on the back of the head. "Yes," I said snippily, "and don't you forget it."

The network brought us lots of contacts and friendships. They went far beyond the borders of Saudi Arabia: and since, as I have already mentioned, there are liberal-minded Saudis living everywhere in the Arab world, and also in Europe, articles for the forum came from those countries too.

Raif was becoming internationally famous. In Lebanon, in Egypt, in Great Britain and in many other countries too there were people who shared his views and corresponded with him through the network. Sometimes they even invited him to conferences. Raif didn't accept many of those offers. But when his friends in Great Britain invited him to visit the island, he couldn't resist: he really looked forward to the trip, as he would meet important people from the liberal scene there.

"You don't mind, do you, Ensaf?" he asked me, with a hint of a guilty conscience in his voice; he had qualms about leaving me alone with the children. A trait that was new to his repertoire. "I won't be more than a week."

"No, you should go!" I answered, since I knew very well how important it was to him. So Raif prepared to travel. The day his flight was due to leave, he was quite jittery with anticipation. "I'm sure it's going to be very exciting," he said to me. "I'll tell you about it every day."

"Promise?"

"I promise," Raif answered and kissed me on the forehead.

Then Turad took him to the airport for his midday flight. I played with the children in the sitting room. Najwa and Dodi had new watercolors, and each of them had a coloring book that they dabbled about in. My little Miriam had just learned to crawl, and clambered eagerly about between them. Fauzia prepared lunch for us in the kitchen. There was an enticing smell of the chickpea soup that was one of her specialities. A shame that Raif wasn't going to be here, because he loved that soup.

After lunch I sat on the couch with the laptop. Raif's plane must have just taken off, I thought. On a whim I looked at the airport's website and entered his flight number. "Departed," it said, as I'd suspected: so Raif was already in the air — and I was a grass widow.

At that moment I heard the sound of a key in the lock of our front door. I flew around, startled. There was a click and the door opened from outside. Someone stepped into the corridor. "Hello!" I heard Raif's voice say. A moment later he came into the sitting room — in exactly the same clothes he'd been wearing when he left the house a few hours before: a white shirt, gray trousers and a jacket. Still, I thought I was seeing a ghost.

"What are you doing here?" I asked, perplexed.

"They won't let me out," he replied dejectedly.

"Who won't let you out?"

"The border guards."

"Why?"

He shrugged. "No idea." Raif threw his jacket over one of the chairs at the dining table and slumped next to me on the sofa.

"But they must have said something," I insisted. "They can't just send you back like that!"

"They told me to report to the court."

"To the court? What's that supposed to mean? What do they want from you?"

"I have no idea. I just know that I'm not allowed to fly to London. I'm not allowed to leave Saudi Arabia." He looked both puzzled and frustrated.

My stomach clenched. Raif having to report to the court could only mean that someone had reported him. And that the crime he was being accused of was very serious. I had a terrible premonition. It could only come from someone in Raif's life. Someone who was more annoyed by Raif's activities than anyone else. Who saw his actions as an affront against himself, and who had already threatened to denounce Raif in the past. But for now I kept my fears to myself.

As soon as Raif had digested his first shock, the next one fluttered into our house in the form of a letter. When Raif read it he turned as white as a sheet. "That's impossible," he stammered, as he stared at the sheet of paper. "What's going on? They can't do that!"

The message came from Raif's bank. It told him all his accounts were frozen, and that with immediate effect he couldn't withdraw any money. No explanation, nothing. Just the renewed instruction to report to the legal authorities.

I looked at Raif. Should I tell him who I suspected? Could I do that? Or would he think I lacked respect? My heart was in my mouth when I broke the taboo and asked my question:

"Raif, my darling, is it possible that your father is behind all this?"

"My father? Why my father?" Raif shook his head. He still didn't want to accept the possibility that the horror of his childhood could be continuing.

Now you might have thought that Raif, as a grown-up, had finally got rid of his father. But unfortunately that wasn't the case: Mohammed Badawi sticks like glue to Raif and his sister. Something keeps him from leaving his children in peace and simply disappearing from their lives.

First it was Raif's sister Samar who had to put up with their father. The reason for this was the Saudi guardianship system that I have mentioned before. If a woman in this country gets divorced, she automatically comes back under her father's wing. From then on he is allowed to make decisions for her. And that was exactly what happened to Samar when her marriage fell apart late in 2005.

I have to admit that I don't know Samar particularly well. She came to my wedding, but we have never been particularly close. I found her a bit brittle, and she probably thought I was too superficial for her brother at the time. Whatever. Perhaps Samar and I were also jealous of each other because we both played an important part in Raif's life and didn't like sharing him. That's why I never inquired too deeply into the background to her divorce.

I just know that afterward Samar was forced to come back, with her little son, to the house of her father, who was still living in Riyadh at the time. She stayed for three years but it must have been an absolute nightmare. Shortly after moving to Jeddah, she fled to a women's crisis center.

This institution, a refuge for women and children, had

only existed for a few years at the time — and only in comparatively worldly Jeddah. Even though I'm sure there were countless towns that needed houses like that, so far this one is unique in the kingdom. Raif helped Samar to flee there and stay hidden from her father.

Mohammed Badawi seethed with fury when the center offered Samar protection, and started a revenge campaign against his children. Against Samar, and against Raif who had helped her. To do this, he returned to a tried and tested method. In 2008 he accused them both of "parental disobedience." The same accusation with which he had once condemned Raif to a kind of hell.

In 2008, alongside that accusation, he launched a smear campaign against his children. At first it seemed rather unprofessional, in fact practically amateurish. It went more or less like this: Abu Raif put on a freshly ironed white shirt and his red checked headdress and sat down on the sofa in his sitting room. Then he handed his mobile phone to a member of his family. While the camera ran he launched into an extravagant tirade about the decline of his two children. He accused Samar of fleeing her legal guardian, himself; where Raif was concerned, he attacked the liberal forum where, he said, the most terrible blasphemy was being practiced. Deep down, Mohammed Badawi is not especially religious. But like many others, he has worked out that from behind the mask of piety you can easily attack others — and he abuses Islam for his own ends.

Then he uploaded those videos onto YouTube. At first no one looked at them. No one was interested in an old man and his ludicrous speeches. They were hidden away somewhere in the depths of the Internet. And if you didn't set out to look for them specifically, you didn't happen upon them. It was only when Raif's network became better known — and in conservative circles more and more unpopular — that the clerics started taking an interest in him and his accusations. They referred to Abu Raif's pronouncements in their own speeches. Might this be the lever that would let them take concrete action against Raif? At any rate, their quotes ensured that the videos became better and better known.

Raif didn't take any of it too seriously. "Come here, Ensaf, take a look at this!" he said, calling me over to him in the sitting room, having come across one of the videos when surfing the web. Raif had put in his own name on YouTube — and what had come out was a video of his father. He reset the recording to the beginning. It showed Abu Raif sitting on his sofa at home as ever. He spoke in an apparently soft, but still subliminally aggressive tone. His small eyes lurked behind a pair of horn-rimmed glasses. I couldn't pay attention to his words, I was so enthralled by the performance. The man was a joke, but he was still terrifying, like a figure in a chamber of horrors.

"He's utterly shameless," said Raif, repelled.

"Could he be a danger to you?"

"Him! To me?" Raif laughed. "What nonsense! His accusations are completely empty." He told me that his father was only so annoyed because he was well aware that he had no power over Samar or over himself. He stroked my cheek and said, "Please don't worry about him."

But after the closure of the bank accounts everything suddenly looked very different. Raif called his lawyer Walid Abu al-Khair, a famous Saudi human rights activist. Walid whistled through his teeth when he found out about the latest developments. "They didn't let you leave — even though your passport is valid?" he asked. "Unbelievable!"

But even he couldn't guess whether it was Raif's political opponents or his father's activities that lay behind the travel ban and the closure of the accounts. Or maybe it was both together. Had they forged an alliance against Raif? Mohammed Badawi's unbounded hatred, coupled with the concentrated political power of the religious establishment: it was a highly explosive mixture. And again he had that vague feeling in his belly.

Walid promised Raif to approach the legal authorities. When he came to our house the next day, he brought bad news. "There's something bigger at work," he said to Raif. "They've taken away your legal status."

"What? What does that mean?"

"You barely exist for the authorities anymore. You have no rights as a citizen of the state," Walid explained.

"But it can't be as simple as that!"

Walid rubbed his nose. He is a short, stocky man with a neat three-day beard and rimless intellectual glasses. Unlike most Saudis, he usually wears western clothes. "Hm, that's what you would think," he said, looking around as if he was worried that somebody might be listening in on the conversation. "But unfortunately we live in Saudi Arabia."

"It's incredible!" said Raif. "What am I supposed to do now?"

Walid asked him to try to be patient. In the meantime we looked for practical solutions to get some sort of hold on my life under the new conditions. Luckily I had two bank accounts that hadn't been closed. That was where we had put most of our money. Raif had always transferred his income to me straightaway. I offered him my credit card with a pretense of condescension. "Be glad you have me," I said jokingly.

"I am, Ensaf. Believe me, I am."

As a family, of course, we faced terrible problems, because our legal representative (which is Raif as the head of the family) could no longer act as an intermediary between us and the authorities. I couldn't even register our little Miriam in our family book (since Raif, her father, did not exist for the authorities anymore). Stripped of our legal existence our whole family led a kind of shadow life. That was why I urged him to take charge of the matter.

But for some reason Raif was reluctant to go on the offensive. In retrospect, I think he was just too scared of confronting the state power. "I would rather you and the children were out of Saudi Arabia when I address this matter," he admitted openly. So he was putting off the problem.

Meanwhile his opponents were drawing up their positions. We learned from Walid that Mohammed Badawi had brought fresh accusations against his children, before a different court this time. "It looks as if we'll have to fight this case so that he will leave you both in peace and you will get your rights back," Walid told him.

Samar, who was still in the women's house in Jeddah, was the first to be brought before the court. I think that perhaps her father saw her as the easier victim. But Samar ignored the summons, and simply didn't turn up for the hearing. In June 2009 the judge, Abdullah al-Uthaim, issued an order for her arrest.

Walid and Raif held a crisis meeting. "If she stays in that women's house it's only a matter of time before they arrest her," said Walid. "You'll have to let her live somewhere else. Maybe at your house?"

"That would be one possibility." Raif looked at me questioningly. I didn't say anything. But I wasn't keen on the idea: Raif and I already had enough problems of our own with the state power. And now on top of everything we were to take in someone facing an arrest warrant? It didn't sound as if it would reduce our problems.

From the concern in Walid's voice I could tell that his client meant a lot to him. Samar is a very beautiful woman. Even if you see just her face, you can't help but notice. Like Raif, she has very light skin, fine, sensitive features and high eyebrows. Walid was probably also taken with her brisk, confident manner. And he was impressed by the way she resisted her tyrannical father. In short: he was smitten with Samar.

"This is the first place they'll look for her," I warned. But no one listened to my objection. So Samar came to our house and stayed until Raif had found her a small flat nearby.

Walid didn't keep his interest in Samar secret for long. He told Raif that he wanted to marry his sister. Raif was enthusiastic about the idea. He really liked Walid, and Samar liked him too. Her problems would also be solved by marriage, and as a wife she would get her respectable status back. There could be no better solution for her.

There was only one obstacle ahead: Mohammed Badawi. As Samar's guardian he had the last word on whether and who she could marry. Needless to say, he got up on his hind legs and strictly refused his agreement. But now Walid went into top gear as a lawyer.

He advised Samar to bring a case against her own father. She should simply turn the tables. Instead of letting him bring a case against her, she should level an accusation against him and put him in the position of having to defend himself against her accusations. Then it would be one accusation against another: father and daughter would be in stalemate.

He had quickly constructed the accusation for her. Under Saudi law there are a few crimes that are unknown anywhere else in the world. That includes the crime of *adhl*: the continuing refusal by a father to grant his daughter permission to marry. Walid, who knew all the legal tricks and loopholes, brought Samar's attention to this possibility. And she sued her father without a moment's hesitation.

In April 2010 Samar was summoned to a legal proceeding because of her accusation of adhl. This time she appeared, to put her father behind bars at last. But she had underestimated him: on the way into the courtroom she herself was arrested. The reason was the case of "parental disobedience" that still hung over her head.

Samar was put in Briman prison in Jeddah. Of course Walid was up in arms about this. He moved heaven and earth to get his fiancée out of jail.

In July 2010 he gained a temporary victory: the governor of the province of Mecca, Khalid bin Faisal al-Saud, suggested calling a committee to reconcile father and daughter. Mohammed Badawi was to let Samar get married and not to bring any more cases against her. But the old man refused to withdraw his accusation. Even when the court found Raif's father guilty in the adhl case the same month, he wouldn't hear of reconciliation. He set all the wheels in motion to ensure that his daughter stayed in jail while he appealed against his own verdict. Meanwhile the NGO founded by Ibrahim al-Mugaiteeb, the Human Rights First Society, which regularly brings human rights cases in the kingdom, publicly declared Samar's imprisonment to be "illegal."

In October 2010 she was finally pardoned by Khalid bin Faisal. The governor appointed an uncle rather than her father as her guardian. He immediately granted her permission to marry. A short time later Samar and Walid got married. Raif's sister was saved.

But Raif's father felt seriously humiliated by his defeat, and behaved like a wounded beast of prey. He made a series of new, appallingly embarrassing videos and uploaded them to the Internet.

The frightening thing about these videos was not so much their content: we already knew the accusations. What was properly alarming was that they were becoming more and more professional from a technical point of view: now Raif's father was suddenly delivering his tirades of hatred in a studio, while being filmed by several cameras. There was money and professional know-how behind the productions, which could only mean that Abu Raif had found influential allies: quite publicly, people from the religious power elite were now waging a campaign. "I hope not too many people will watch this crap," said Raif, when he had happened on one of the videos in which his father insulted him and his sister. It had had several hundred "likes." "We can't pursue this dispute in the public eye."

But that was exactly what Abu Raif wanted — and his profile was growing by the day.

"Hey, Raif, I saw your father on television," a friend said to him one day. "He doesn't have a good word to say about you."

"Where on television?" asked Raif. "Which program would that have been?"

His friend told him the name of an ultrareligious private satellite broadcaster that we didn't normally watch. His father had appeared on it the previous day, talking about Raif. "Take a look," the friend said. "It's really worth seeing. You ought to know what he's saying about you."

In the evening Raif looked up the program on YouTube. He sat with his laptop on the sofa in our sitting room. I sat down beside him, because I was curious as well.

It was a talk show. The guests were Raif's father, his younger brother Abdel-Illah and a number of guests, ultra-conservative politicians and imams. The presenter also had a religious appearance: he wore the goatee beard of the fundamentalist Salafists, a reference to his worldview which anyone in Saudi Arabia knows how to interpret. All the men on the show wore the keffiyeh headdress fastened with the *agal*, a kind of black headband, and the long white *thobe*, the traditional Saudi uniform. It looked almost as if they were competing for the most devout-looking outfit.

"Now tell us what has happened," the presenter said to Raif's father.

He began to deliver a long speech. An accusation in which he listed in detail his two children's crimes. He spoke about his daughter Samar as if she were an object, a possession that had been unjustly taken away from him. He declared her marriage to Walid to be invalid, since they had been married without his permission. "I'm her father," he said, "she belongs to me. But she has been stolen from me."

"That is a serious matter," the presenter confirmed. "And what part did your son play in that?"

Raif's father accused him of making common cause with Walid. "My son is a renegade," he said. "He runs a liberal net-work and has dealings with liberal fellows like this Walid Abu al-Khair." He spoke the name with distinct revulsion — and in such a way that the last part of it, which actually means "the good," could also be misunderstood as "the evil."

"He defends him in his writings. But 'liberal' simply means that these people have abandoned the Islamic faith."

A general nod among the guests. "God help us," one of them murmured.

"The brains of my two children were incorrectly formatted," Raif's father raged. "Like a computer hard drive, filled with ideas that are alien to Saudi society." He then quite openly announced his desire to be there when they were both justly punished in public. Implicitly he meant the death sentence, which is usually applied in our country for the crime of apostasy, or loss of faith.

"I call upon the king, the emirs and all the scholars to help me in this matter," said Raif's father. "Where are you all? Why is no one seeing to it that the law is finally upheld? Have the liberals already assumed power in our country?"

We watched the program from start to finish. Then Raif snapped his laptop shut. "It's enough to make you ill," he said irritably. I tried to find his hand. When I touched it, his fingers were cold and damp. Then I knew that the whole thing had affected him more deeply than he wanted to show me.

"If he manages to persuade the right people, his accusations could become very dangerous," I said. "Couldn't they?"

"I hope not. Nobody's going to believe that kind of nonsense! Or are they?"

He sounded far from convinced. I raised my eyebrows. Neither of us had any idea about how to deal with the new accusations we were facing. The whole story was slowly becoming a real public scandal.

I was extremely uncomfortable with Raif's father's accusations. I was ashamed to have a father-in-law like that. What would the neighbors think when they saw him on television? And his grandchildren when they found out about it?

One morning our phone rang. Raif picked up. The editor of a state television program was on the line. "We've planned a talk show with your father for this evening," he told Raif—who looked at me and rolled his eyes with annoyance: not again! "I wanted to ask if you'd like to take part in the program."

At first I shook my head, horrified. "No, I don't think so," Raif replied politely.

"So why are you so implacable?" the editor said provocatively.

"I'm not, but..."

"You see! Perhaps there's a way for the two of you to make peace on the program."

He persuaded Raif, who eventually said yes. As soon as he had put the phone down he regretted his decision. And I too thought it wasn't a good idea to wash the family's dirty laundry live before the eyes of the whole television-watching nation. "Then at least get some support," I advised Raif. "Invite Walid for dinner tonight."

He did. And Walid immediately agreed. In the end it was his reputation and the reputation of his wife that were at stake. When the time had come, the two men sat in front of the television. I brought them crisps and Coca-Cola. We banished the children to another room so that they didn't make a noise when the producer rang to speak to him live on air. And I didn't want them to hear their grandfather saying such horrible things on television. Where the two older ones were concerned we couldn't be sure if they would even recognize the man. They had only met him briefly once when they were smaller. So I put them — under loud protests from Najwa and Dodi — in the care of Fauzia.

I myself joined Raif and Walid in the sitting room. The discussion on television was already in full swing. Like the previous time, the talk show *Al Diwaniyat al-Dana*, the Al-Dana Salon, was about our private family matters, Samar's marriage first of all. The clerics were accusing Raif of fraternizing with Walid.

"Why don't we just ask the accused themselves," said the presenter, and for a moment he enjoyed the embarrassment that his suggestion spread among the guests. A moment later the phone that I had put on the sitting-room table rang. Raif answered.

"Yes?" he said.

"Ready?" asked a program assistant.

"Of course."

"I hear that Raif Badawi, the son of Mohammed Raif Badawi, is joining us on the line. You will probably know him as the editor of the 'Saudi Liberal Network.' Can you hear us, Mr. Badawi?"

"Loud and clear," said Raif.

"Fantastic! What do you have to say about the accusation?"

"My sister married completely legally. Her father wasn't present, that is correct. But her uncle, to whom guardianship had been transferred at that point, was present, and so was I. Their marriage was concluded according to the laws of Islam."

"That's a lie!" shouted Raif's father on television. He leaped to his feet, his face scarlet with rage.

"Calm down, Father," said Raif's younger brother Abdel-Illah, who was with him on the program. He is a delicate young man with fine features like Raif's, but he is completely under his father's sway. "If you'll let me, I'll answer Raif."

The presenter nodded in agreement.

"Walid Abu al-Khair is a foreign agent," Abdel-Illah said in a deep voice of great conviction. "He and Raif belong to a gang that has lost its faith and wants to damage our state with its atheist network."

Raif and Walid looked at each other, shaking their heads with disbelief as they listened to his words. And I too thought I wasn't hearing properly. Had he lost his mind, making such a claim? How many hundreds of thousands of people all over Saudi Arabia were watching this prime-time show?

"Walid has planned this long in advance. And you, Raif, helped him in his criminal act. I have concrete proof of this," said Raif's brother, and waved a piece of paper in front of the camera. "Together you have persuaded Samar that she is a victim of domestic violence!"

"I hear that Mr. Abu al-Khair is present as well," the presenter interrupted. "This is a great opportunity for you to put forth your side of the story."

Raif passed the phone to Walid. "Good evening. In fact it's all been said already," he said, and his voice was transmitted live to the studio. Again he listed the reasons why his wedding to Samar had been legitimate.

"Lies! Lies!" her father yelled over and over again. "The girl Samar isn't your wife!"

"Is it true that Samar was abused by her father?" the presenter asked Walid.

"I don't want to say anything about her father." Although

the dispute was getting down to the bone, Walid was still reluctant to say anything disrespectful about his wife's father. That's how important respect for parents and parents-in-law is in our country. "But an independent witness has confirmed as much."

"Yes, her uncle," Raif's father replied. "But he doesn't count, because he's another liberal traitor."

"Did Raif deliver liberal speeches even as a child?" one of the guests on the panel wanted to know. "On his network he makes fun of religion today."

"Heaven forbid! I would have forbidden it!"

"*Al-hamdulillah* — you're telling the truth at last," Raif said, commenting on his father's words down the line.

"As editor of the network he had a duty to prevent slander against religion!"

"Yes, absolutely!" "Exactly so!" Suddenly everyone in the studio was talking at the same time.

Walid tried to calm the talk-show guests. "Let's not get everything muddled up," he said. "This family dispute has absolutely nothing to do with the liberal network."

"Indeed it does!" barked Raif's father.

"Come and join us in the studio next week," said the moderator to Walid.

"No," said Walid. "Mohammed Badawi is my wife's father and I don't want to talk about him. Whatever he does. It's a private matter for us."

Raif's father had no such scruples. "I hope you'll soon rot in jail with your friend Hamsa al-Kashgari!" he shouted. Al-Kashgari, a political friend of Walid and Raif's, had just been extradited from Malaysia and locked up in Saudi Arabia for supposedly slandering our prophet in a tweet. "I don't like your halo; I won't pray to you," he had written. A hot political issue at the time, the case was on everyone's lips.

"I repeat: let's not mix everything up," Walid pleaded with the panel. "This is a family dispute. And it is wrong to turn it into a battle between liberals and orthodox Muslims."

Raif's father saw his words as a gift. "But that's exactly the reality!" he announced. "I am engaged in a battle against the liberals. And I challenge all right-thinking Muslims to support me in that struggle!"

The conservative cleric applauded Raif's father for his performance. The clerics were impressed with him for wanting to call his wayward son to his senses. Many of them had words of praise for the initiative and offered him their support.

We, on the other hand, were very concerned about the absurd turn the dispute between father and son had just taken — and how many allies Mohammed had been able to find in a relatively short time. Cranking up his personal thirst for revenge into a battle between conservatives and liberals in Saudi Arabia had been a brilliant move. It gave his campaign a huge and menacing dynamic, particularly in reference to Raif. Samar had been able to get herself a little out of the firing line through her counteraccusation and her marriage to Walid. But Raif was vulnerable: the liberal network made him an easy and welcome target for the clergy.

After the program Raif felt the air around him getting thinner. In his blogs and articles, however, he didn't tone his words down, but instead became increasingly explicit. States based on religion kept people "in an eternal loop of fear," Raif wrote — as if writing away his own anxieties.

"Anyone who observes Arab society will see in a spectacular way how it groans, moans and suffers under the burden of theocracy whose clerics want to hear nothing but the words 'I hear and I obey,' he said on *Al Hiwar Almotamadin* (Civilized dialogue). "In fact it is beyond dispute that Arab society has such religious loyalty to the clergy that it is possible for their fatwas and interpretations to become the absolute, indeed the sacred truth. And no sooner does a free spirit come along than he sees himself confronted with a surge of hundreds of fatwas that the clerics compete with one another to pass, in order to declare him an unbeliever and threaten him just because he has disputed that sacredness."

If I think back to those texts now, it almost seems to me as if he saw his own fate coming. Perhaps it was that premonition, his secret suspicion that he would have little time left to formulate his thoughts and communicate them to the world, that made him more and more productive — and also more and more provocative.

In that last phase his theoretical engagement was governed by the concept of liberalism. Raif understood the term to mean tolerance on the part of the state and respect for the individual freedom of its citizens. He expressed the idea very concisely with the motto "live and let live." A kind of maxim, for which he argued vehemently. For him it also included the right to religious freedom. "According to liberalism, religions are nothing but personal decisions," he wrote. "The liberal state is a state without religion. Which isn't to say that it is atheist, but rather that it preserves the rights of all religions, encourages and supports them, without discrimination or preference of one religion over another, without placing the faith of the majority above other religions."

That was too much for our imams. To put Islam on the same footing as other religions, as Raif had done in countless blogs, was considered sacrilegious. And with his plea for a separation of state and religion, Raif made many more enemies. Because in our country secularism is equated with godlessness. Such statements are simply taboo. Of course Raif knew that he was taking a great risk. But he couldn't help it: he had to say what he had to say.

One evening, I think it was in autumn 2011, I found him sitting pale and very still on the sofa with his laptop. The children were scribbling beside him, or playing catch in the sitting room. But he wasn't paying them any attention. It struck me as odd. "What's up, Raif?" I asked him.

"Oh, nothing." He opened his mouth and closed it again. Then for a while he stared past his computer into the void. Something had happened, but he wouldn't tell me what.

In the evening he helped me put the children to bed. They liked to snuggle up, all three of them together, on a big mattress. Raif waited until they had gone to sleep. Then he quietly lay down beside them and hugged them from behind, again without a word. I would see that gesture often in the months that followed.

"What's up, Raif?" I repeated when we had both gone to bed. "Please tell me."

"Oh," he fidgeted around. "It isn't really anything special. It's those imams again, making a stink."

This wasn't a new problem: one of them was constantly criticizing the network.

"Who is it this time?"

"That guy Abdulrahman al-Barrak."

"Al-Barrak, al-Barrak...?" I had a feeling I knew the name from somewhere.

"He and a bunch of his friends have written an online petition against me."

"They probably have nothing better to do!"

"Apparently not." He kissed me. "Don't worry, nothing's going to happen."

The next day I tried to find al-Barrak on the Internet. He's an old hand in the Saudi clergy. That was why his name seemed so familiar: three years ago, I read, he had demanded the death of two journalists with the *al-Riyadh* newspaper, because they had supposedly published blasphemous articles. And some time before he had made death threats against anyone who advocated the equality of the sexes, since that supposedly contravened Sharia law. It didn't sound good.

Worried, I looked up Raif's forum, where such subjects were always discussed in detail. I looked through the articles for the cleric's name — and found it immediately: he had even made it into the headlines. Right beside the name al-Barrak I noticed a word that frightened me to death: "Fatwa."

Had the imam delivered a legal opinion? About Raif? He'd never mentioned it to me!

The text of the articles confirmed my worst premonitions: yes, clearly al-Barrak had written an opinion. And he had reached the conclusion that Raif was a *murtad*, a renegade who had lost his faith. An apostate.

I felt dizzy when I read that. I had to hold on to my chair. I stared at the screen as if hypnotized. I found a link that led directly to the text of the judgment. It first listed a few points demonstrating precisely why Raif had to be seen as an apostate, and then said in conclusion: "The author of these statements, who lives among Muslims and hears the Qur'an, is an unbeliever. And since he belongs to Islam, these statements make him a renegade. So this must be borne in mind and he must be brought to book for his statements."

The author also refused to accept the excuses that Raif had given in his defense. To support his position he quoted sura 9 of the Qur'an, verses 65 and 66: "If you ask them, what were you talking about, they are sure to say: 'We were just talking and playing about.' Say: 'Were you making fun of God and his signs and his prophets? Don't apologize! You became disbelievers after being believers! If we forgive one group of you, we will punish another for being criminals.'"

Al-Barrak demanded the death penalty for Raif. Overall, 150 clerics had joined in with his devastating judgment and signed it on the Internet.

It was carte blanche for religious fanatics: anyone who had murderous thoughts about Raif or who wanted to do something to him was thus justified in advance of the crime. I knew that many radical Salafists would take the cleric's words as an invitation to vigilantism.

My first impulse was to call Raif and ask him to come home straightaway. But I didn't want to worry him even more. So I controlled myself. When he arrived home in the evening, I was waiting for him at the door and hugged him in silence. Now that I had understood the scale of the disaster, I was the one who found herself unable to speak. I didn't want to show him how scared I was. We both felt the same.

"How can a man who doesn't know you claim that you're a disbeliever?" was all I asked him. "What gives him the right to judge the relationship between you and your God?"

Raif shook his head helplessly. "That's one of the many mysteries that our country presents us with."

We didn't talk much about the subject, so as not to give

it any more power over our lives than it had already. But I noticed the change in Raif's behavior: he was silent, thoughtful, almost a little depressed. He carefully locked all the doors, and never liked leaving the house on his own.

Often he watched Najwa, Dodi and little Miriam sleeping. "If something happens to me, you have to be strong for the children, Ensaf," he once said to me. I didn't want to hear things like that. He also gave me the number of a friend I was to contact if anything happened to him. "He'll help you," he said.

Usually I ignored such things. "Stop it! What are you talking about?" I interrupted him, and then quickly tried to change the subject. "Do you fancy watching a film with me?" I couldn't bear the idea of someone hurting Raif.

By now he was spending more and more time at home. I don't mean he was hiding, but it was a bit like that: too many people knew him, and too many people hated him. He didn't want to make himself a target for some lunatic by constantly appearing in the outside world.

There was also the fact that his job wasn't going particularly well. The employment agency for women had been a financial flop. After that Raif had tried to set up two more English institutes, both with only moderate financial success. Now he was unemployed. Because of his still vague legal situation he had no hope of a job with the state or in a company. As I've said, he didn't even have a bank account—and now he didn't have a valid passport, either. It was already hard enough to transfer the fees that editors paid for his articles into my account.

So we lived mostly on our savings. For Raif, who has a very generous character and always likes to invite all the people around him to our house, it wasn't easy. He hated asking his friends for support when he was no longer able, on his own, to pay the cost of the server on which his network ran. And that was three thousand dollars a month.

Things were a bit easier for me. I didn't protest when we moved to a smaller flat. Or when I had to fire my maid. That was just how it was. I must even say that I have very good memories of that last, tiny flat, because Raif and I were so close during that time. That was the most important thing for me.

Of course life is more fun when you don't have to count every last cent. I wasn't used to thinking too hard when the children wanted a particular toy or needed new clothes; they were growing so quickly. After all, I had always had everything I wanted. This was a big change.

We spent a lot less on restaurants, as we hardly went out for reasons of safety. On the other hand we had lots of visitors to our little flat. Every Friday evening we had a kind of "open sitting room" for our friends. Raif invited journalists, writers and other authors who were active in the network. Between ten and twenty activists, both male and female, came regularly to our house. Over tea, coffee and cakes served by our porter's wife, we read out articles, poems and other publications, and talked about the current political subjects, sometimes until midnight.

I really liked the atmosphere at those meetings. The people were interesting, spirited, with inspiring ideas. The women didn't veil themselves to the point that you couldn't recognize them; most of them just loosely draped a scarf over their heads. And when they wore abayas, they were prettily decorated ones that looked like clothes. Not like tents. I generally joined them wearing jeans and a blouse, covering my hair with a brightly colored silk scarf. I didn't speak much at those meetings myself, but I liked to listen to the others.

I also met the cofounder of the network, Souad, on one such occasion. A woman of over forty, who already had grown-up children, she is the first woman lawyer in Saudi Arabia, and I was very impressed by her. I hadn't met women who were so intellectual and well-read before. I was especially struck by how confidently and commandingly she talked to the men about political subjects. And how respectfully they treated her. Almost as if she were a man as well.

Events in Tunisia and Egypt were, of course, the subject of especially heated discussion: what seemed at the time to be the very hopeful start of the so-called Arab Spring. The friends argued about whether these uprisings in neighboring countries might herald similar events in Saudi Arabia, and what might come afterward.

In his articles Raif declared the Islamic model a failure. "The show is bleak," he mocked, "so lower the curtain so that we can discuss the matter in all its breadth." He argued for looking at other models, including the western one: "If a thinker, whatever his rank and his importance, simply comes along and says the purely western model of secularism doesn't represent a solution, he is opening the gate to hell."

But in the end he was convinced that none of the models already known could be applied to Arab societies, and we had to develop something completely autonomous in our own cultural circle. Something that hadn't existed before. After all, the revolutionaries of the French Revolution hadn't looked for models in history, he argued. "We haven't even started. We will only start when we are clearly aware that we need to start neither where our peers have stopped nor where our predecessors started. We have to start where we have to start: from the very beginning."

I was pleased to notice how impressed our guests were by writing like this. At such moments I was really proud of Raif. Who else had a husband who could put his thoughts into words so brilliantly?

Of course, things weren't always easy: sometimes the money quite honestly wasn't enough for the children's kindergarten and private school. But Raif had done great things. He had founded a network in which all the authors and thinkers of Saudi Arabia were able to exchange ideas. Our country's intellectual elite was sitting on our sofa. They were our friends, and came and went in and out of our house. Wasn't that worth even more?

Yes, what was it worth—everything that Raif had achieved? What price would we end up paying for it? A few inconveniences, a smaller flat? Yes, of course. The right to own a passport and leave the country whenever we wanted? We had given up those privileges as well. Was that enough? What else were they going to want from us? I thought about Raif's father's pending lawsuit. About the fatwa. No, that wasn't yet enough, I sensed: our enemies didn't know about "live and let live." They wouldn't rest until they had destroyed us completely.

Soon after Abdulrahman al-Barrak's petition was published on the Internet, there was a problem with the website. I was sitting in the car with Raif after my Zumba class when he found out. Once a week, when the children were in school and at kindergarten, I went with the women from the neighborhood to a fitness studio, one of the few to have been opened in Jeddah. There, hidden behind high walls, we rocked out, in bright neon tops and under the instruction of a Latina trainer, to Brazilian funk. I thought it was enormous fun. I was always completely pumped and happy when—again severely swathed in black—I got into Raif's Peugeot to go and pick up the children. But this time I noticed that he was nervous and distracted. His mobile phone kept ringing: something was up with the network.

"When we try to call up the forum, everything on the screen is blank," callers were saying.

"Could you check?"

"Yes, in half an hour," Raif promised. "I'm on my way."

When we got home, he immediately sat down at the computer. Of course the forum was his home page. When he clicked on his browser, the page seemed to appear. But then the image changed: "WE WILL KILL YOU!" it said, in bright red letters.

Raif, who was sitting at our dining-room table, involuntarily pushed his chair back slightly. He looked around for me. I was a little way behind him. When I saw his face I knew straightaway that something strange was going on. I came closer. Before Raif could stop me, I put on my glasses. I read the text: the death threat. Below the big scarlet letters, in a slightly smaller font, there was a quotation from some sura from the Qur'an. But quite honestly I can't remember which one it was.

"They won't stop," Raif said flatly.

"No, of course not. What are you going to do?"

Raif took out his phone and photographed the page. Then he dialed the number of a friend who was a computer expert.

His friend confirmed that the website had been hacked. Raif asked him to get it up and running again as soon as possible.

He was on top of the problem after a few hours. When the page could be opened normally again, there were a lot of people asking what had happened. Some of the more active members assumed that the government had temporarily closed the site down. But Raif told them all it was the work of hackers. He published in his blog the photograph with the death threat, which had only appeared on his own screen.

After that the phone didn't stop ringing. All our friends were extremely concerned. They rang us and asked if they could do anything. But the problem is that when something like that happens there's basically nothing you can do. You feel terribly helpless. But you just have to go on living as before as far as possible, without being influenced or intimidated by what's happened. If you can't sleep at night, you get a prescription for tranquilizers.

That death threat wouldn't be the only one. After this there was a time when the intimidating messages came in almost daily. Mostly they rang Raif on his phone. We weren't sure if it was always the same caller or several different ones. The forum was repeatedly hacked too—but in such a way that only Raif could see the messages. Often he showed them to me: some were simply wild insults in the language of the gutter, but there were also actual threats to kill him.

"Look how angry these people are," Raif said. "This is what our country has come to."

Those guttersnipes didn't spare me either: they told Raif they owned naked photographs of me. They would publish them on the forum if he didn't take it off the Net straightaway. We could only laugh about that. "No one has any naked photographs of me," I reassured my husband.

Things got darker when they told us they had stolen pictures of the children from our hard drive, and were going to post them on the web. "Is that even possible?" I asked Raif.

"Sure," he said. "But I think they're bluffing." For the sake of caution he put all our private data on an external storage device and deleted it from his hard drive. "That way we'll be more protected against viral attacks."

The fact that they were now aiming at the whole family, not stopping even at the children, touched us at our most sensitive point. Would we be able to protect them well enough? The two older ones were already going to school, and the little one was at a private kindergarten. Who knew what could happen there!

"Perhaps you and the children should go away for a while," Raif suggested, "until things have calmed down here."

I didn't think it was a bad idea. I've always liked traveling. Our political friends had already offered to give us financial support. But the idea of Raif not coming with me stung my heart. He still couldn't leave the country because of his travel ban.

"By ourselves?" I asked him.

"It would only be for a while." He promised me to pursue his case with the authorities and clarify his legal status as soon as we were out of the firing line. "If I knew there was nothing they could do to you I would feel safer; I could fight in quite a different way."

It was an important argument, but I didn't find it convincing. I couldn't leave Raif alone in that terrible situation. I wouldn't have a single calm moment with the children if I didn't know what was happening to him. No, I wanted to stay in Jeddah, with Raif. Our family wouldn't be torn apart.

"Think about it," he said. And we deferred the discussion.

With all that stress we couldn't sleep particularly well. Often we spent the whole night watching television. We deliberated — or just tried to distract ourselves from the oppressive reality by zapping through the channels.

On one of those evenings I suddenly felt terribly hungry. I desperately needed a snack, crisps or nuts. It was already ten or eleven o'clock. But in Saudi Arabia many supermarkets are open until midnight, including the one in our neighborhood that we normally went to.

"I don't suppose you could go out and get us something?" I asked Raif. Perhaps that was a bit mean, because I know he can never deny me such requests.

He immediately put on his shoes and looked for his car key. "What would you like?"

"Something you like too. And maybe a Red Bull," I said, placing my order.

"I'll be right back." He kissed me and disappeared through the front door.

Raif, my Raif. How could I have known that I was sending him into the arms of a potential murderer?

While I waited at home in front of the television, Raif drove to the supermarket in our rattly old Peugeot. He parked it in the big car park in front of the shopping center, which was still very busy even though it was so late. In Saudi Arabia people tend to go to bed late. On his way to the sales hall he stopped off at an ATM, as he had run out of money again. He put my card in the slot and entered his PIN. Then he heard screams behind him.

He turned around and saw the flash of a knife. A man with a dark, curly beard was running at him. Luckily other passers-by had spotted the assailant. A man managed to grab him and throw him to the ground.

General tumult broke out. "Let go of me!" the man yelled as if possessed, lying on the ground. "Let me give this unbeliever the punishment he deserves."

The men in front of the supermarket conferred with one another. No one paid any attention to Raif, who was in complete shock.

While the men were still arguing about whether the attacker was right or wrong — and what to do with him — Raif went back to his car as if on remote control, sat down behind the wheel and drove straight home.

When I opened the door to him, he was white with fear, and his whole body was shaking.

"What's up, Raif?" I asked in alarm. "What's wrong? Has something happened?"

"I nearly died," he whispered quietly, as if he himself didn't want to hear the truth. He pulled me onto the sofa and hugged me for a few minutes without saying anything. Then he told me what had happened outside the supermarket.

I couldn't believe it. "Curse a country that produces such monsters," I said furiously.

He nodded. "Ensaf," he said. "Please, do me a favor. Take the children and get out of here."

# CHAPTER FIVE

# A JOURNEY INTO THE UNKNOWN

L eaving the country. Leaving my husband behind. Raif and I talked for a long time about whether this was the right step. There were two things to weigh up: our safety and our financial options.

Where safety was concerned, Raif shared my opinion. There was no room for argument: the attempted murder had shown both of us how serious the situation was. We could no longer ignore the danger, particularly for the sake of our children. Because who knew what those lunatics would come up with next? We had to get those innocent little creatures out of the firing line. Neither Raif nor I could bear the idea that they might become the victim of our problems.

We also had to think about what would become of them if something happened to their father. Then our families would inevitably appear on the scene. I would be placed under the guardianship of my father, who would also be given the right to bring up the children. I didn't want that. But the other option was even worse: Abu Raif could claim the right to bring them up — and as paternal grandfather he had an even better chance of getting it. Unthinkable!

The horrific scenario of Abu Raif taking charge of our three children was quite honestly what made me yield to Raif's wish. I saw no other chance: the children and I had to get out of the country.

But our financial means were now very modest. We didn't even have enough money for airline tickets, let alone a long stay abroad. Expensive countries like Malaysia were completely out of the question. We had to be pragmatic. Egypt seemed to be a possible alternative: the rents and school costs for the children were almost bearable there. And it was an Arab country where we knew the language and where it would be easier for Raif, when he came and joined us, to find a job.

He promised me, hand on heart, that he would be with us as soon as he had sorted out his legal affairs: "Before you find a flat and register the children for school, I'll be with you."

We also discussed the matter with our liberal friends. Almost all of them advised us to leave. After the attempt on Raif's life they were very concerned about us. When they learned that we had problems financing our project, they got together and discussed how they might give us a hand.

There were some very affluent people who were active in the forum and shared Raif's liberal views. They even included emirs and other dignitaries. At one of our Friday meetings a wealthy businessman took Raif aside. I'm not allowed to mention his name, as it might cause him difficulties. Let's just call him Abdol. He's a tall, stately man with a dark mustache and a slightly chubby face.

"Raif," he said when they were alone. "I would like to help you and your family. It's very important for your wife and children to leave the country; you can't wait any longer. If you'll let me, I would like to buy you tickets and finance your first few months in Egypt."

Ashamed, Raif looked at the floor. All of a Saudi man's pride derives from his ability to look after his family well and ensure their safety. That was why the offer was so terribly embarrassing to him. On the other hand he knew that he wouldn't be able to protect us without the help of our friends. And he loved us too much to sacrifice us to his circumstances. So he overcame his reluctance.

"That's a very generous offer," he said to Abdol. "I'll pay you back the money as quickly as possible."

"That won't be necessary."

"I insist."

Just two days later Abdol slipped the cash into Raif's hand. It was sixteen thousand dollars. Raif immediately bought tickets for Cairo; he handed me the rest in an envelope. "I know it's not much," he said, embarrassed. "But it'll be enough to get by for the first little while. And after that I'll be there."

"Yes. Don't worry about it," I said, to inspire confidence. "The children and I will just be having a holiday for a while until you've sorted everything out."

That was exactly how we explained the matter to Najwa, Dodi and little Miriam: they were going on holiday with Mum for a while. Dad would come later, as he had work to do. The children were enthusiastic. They immediately started planning their holidays. "Will we see the Pyramids?" Dodi asked me excitedly. "And go inside them?" He had just seen the film *The Mummy*—and redesigned our sitting room accordingly. He had hung blankets over our dining table to turn it into a pyramid, in which our young explorer risked his life on a tour of discovery, ably assisted by his trusty sisters. Of course Dodi dreamed of unearthing hidden treasure in those old grave chambers. At least that would have solved our financial problems.

"Of course," I promised. "And we'll also explore their secret passageways if the Pharaoh's ghost allows."

He opened his eyes wide. With his shoulder-length curly hair and soft brown eyes he looked like a miniature version of his father. I was greatly comforted by the fact that at least this little Raif would be coming with me. And his sisters too, of course.

While the children got excited about their forthcoming holiday, Raif and I were more thoughtful. But of course we tried not to let it show. We were glad of their unselfconsciousness, and didn't want to burden them with any worries.

I became aware of my own uncertainty when I was packing: what do you put in your bag when you aren't sure if you'll ever come back? The most valuable things, I thought at first — and packed my best clothes as well as my remaining jewelry. When it was full, I realized that I hadn't yet packed a single item of clothing for the children, or any everyday clothes for me.

There was no way that I would be able to get everything else in my second suitcase. So I unpacked it all again and tried to approach the matter more systematically: I would take clothes for one or two months — the length of time that Raif and I had estimated as the maximum for our separation. After that, when he joined us, he could bring the rest of our things. Or else we would go back to Saudi Arabia.

The day of our departure came far too fast. I hadn't slept

all night, but I tried to spread a good mood. "Yoohoo, off we go!" I told the children as I got them ready for the journey. Each of the children, even Miriam, carried their own little rucksack, which Raif put in the boot along with my two big cases.

He drove us to the airport in our rattly Peugeot. Through the eye-slit of my niqab I watched the glittering façades drifting past us. Would I ever see the city again? I had told Najwa and Dodi's school that I had to go abroad for work and would educate the children privately for a while. They would sit their exams at the end of the school year, in April, about four months away. As it was a private school this was easily possible.

However it was just a loophole that I was holding open for myself: in fact I fully expected that Raif would be with us in a few weeks, and that I would then enroll them in an Egyptian school.

"Look, we're nearly at the airport!" said Raif.

The children cheered in the back seat. Najwa and Dodi, who had very vague memories of our trip to Malaysia, were particularly looking forward to the flight. "Is it true that we'll be flying as high as the clouds?" Dodi asked his father.

"Even higher," Raif replied. "Almost as high as the sun."

Dodi clapped his hands enthusiastically. "But you've got to come too, Dad!"

"I'll be with you very, very soon," Raif promised his son.

He lifted our luggage out of the boot, loaded it onto a trolley and accompanied us to the check-in desks. Our three little holidaymakers danced excitedly around us. I went rather reluctantly, as if to draw out the time when we were still together as a family, even though it was just a few minutes.

Before security control Raif hugged each of us individually. He was allowed to kiss the children, but not me, here, in public. "You'll manage," he whispered to me.

"Of course I'll manage," I said, trying to sound stronger than I actually felt. But generally speaking I was confident: it was the right step. Soon we would be leading a normal life in Egypt, all five of us.

"I love you," said Raif.

"I love you too."

I pushed the children toward the security guards. Before they went through the scanners they turned around and waved to him again. Raif waved back. He blew me a kiss. I tried to smile—and was glad that my veil, which I normally hated, hid my tears from him and the children.

When the plane took off, I felt the burden of responsibility weighing on my shoulders. Now I was thrown back entirely on my own resources. I had to be strong for my three children.

In Egypt we were received like guests of state. Raif had asked a very influential friend to help us, a Saudi citizen whose identity, once again, I am unable to reveal. This friend sent his driver to pick us up from the airport. He brought us in a big black Mercedes to the man's property in the middle of Cairo.

The children and I were pretty amazed when we drove through the gate. What we saw was more or less a castle. Behind high walls you couldn't see over from the street there was a big house with a garden that was almost the size of a park. It was beautiful and well-tended. The lawn looked as if it had been mown with a ruler. Flowers bloomed everywhere. Thanks to a sprinkler system that constantly sprayed them with water, all the plants flourished magnificently in this little paradise.

My children looked around in delight: they had never experienced such opulent gardens in Jeddah. They would have run off straightaway to charge about on the lawn and stand in the spray of the sprinkler system. I was only able to stop them with a few firm instructions. Once again I was glad that we had brought them up lovingly, but also encouraged obedience. We moved into a room in a guesthouse a little way from the main building. We were to stay out of sight. As our host was on an official mission in Cairo, our presence could have caused him difficulties.

"It is good that you have come, madame," said our patron when he greeted us in person that evening. "I'm a great admirer of your husband."

"Thank you for helping our family," I said solemnly. I was still rather shy, as I wasn't used to speaking on behalf of our family. And to a man I didn't know. Raif had always assumed that role.

"It's an honor," he stressed. "I hope you feel at home in my house. Mr. H"—the driver—"will help you with everything else."

I thanked him many times over.

"Is everything all right?" Raif asked when he called me in the evening. I was very glad to hear his voice.

"Everything's fine," I reassured him. "We're in good hands."

"I miss you."

"We miss you more."

I gave the children the phone. "It's brilliant here, Dad," Najwa reported. "When are you coming?"

"Soon, sweetie," he promised.

Over the next few days I went with Mr. H in search of a place to live. I was able to leave my children with his wife. He drove me from one viewing to another, crisscrossing the city.

How different Cairo was from Jeddah, I thought as I considered the seething bustle from behind the darkened windows of the air-conditioned Mercedes. In my home country there was essentially no life in the streets: everyone drove around in their expensive cars. Apart from highways, high walls and glass façades there was little to catch the eye. Egypt is a real contrast to that bleakness: here all life takes place in the street. Fascinated, I looked at the many fruit-sellers praising their wares; shoeshine boys loudly calling to their customers; the proprietors of kiosks setting out the day's newspapers; tourist guides with red umbrellas, channeling hordes of white-skinned Europeans through the alleys of the old town from museum to museum. The country was poorer; you could tell by looking at the people. But it was also more colorful, and life was somehow more interesting.

The political situation was confused, however: President Mubarak, who had ruled the country like a king for three decades, had been toppled at the beginning of 2011. Raif and I had avidly followed the news of the protests, which had broken out first in Tunisia and shortly afterward in Egypt, on satellite television. We were pretty amazed at the time, and delighted at how quickly the authoritarian regimes in both countries had unraveled. After only a few weeks the people had chased the despots who governed them out of office.

The protest movement spread like wildfire throughout the whole of the Arab world: soon the Libyans, Syrians, Jordanians and Bahrainis were demonstrating as well. The spark even seemed to jump briefly to Saudi Arabia. Near my home town of Jizan a sixty-five-year-old man set fire to himself. And in Jeddah people protested spontaneously after heavy rainfall in January flooded the city and killed ten people. There were also smaller demonstrations in Qatif, Riyadh, Hofuf and Awamijah. "This is the start," Raif rejoiced at the time.

But in mid-March, when a few brave people planned a nationwide "day of anger," the Saudi security forces intervened: one of the main organizers, Faisal Ahmed Abdul-Ahad, was murdered shortly before the planned event. Rather than the 26,000 people who had joined his Facebook group, only a few hundred dared to take to the streets in Qatif and Hofuf. The police ruthlessly laid into them and nipped their protest in the bud. Some arrests followed. The population fearfully ducked away.

Raif and I were very disappointed that the Arab Spring had come to such a sudden end in Saudi Arabia. But in the other countries, too, the political situation no longer looked very hopeful at the end of the year. The Libyans had succeeded in removing their dictator, Gaddafi, but the various tribes and militias were fighting one another. In Yemen, too, President Saleh, who had ruled for many years, agreed to step down. But in Jordan King Abdullah II had taken control of the situation again by sacrificing his prime minister and his cabinet. And in Bahrain the protest of the majority Shi'ite population had been silenced with the help of Saudi tanks. In Syria the people were still fighting against Bashar al-Assad. But pessimists predicted that the country would splinter into a civil war.

After the swift success of the revolution in my host country of Egypt, the question arose of who would assume lasting power. The religious and the liberal factions were fighting one another. Mohammed Morsi of the Muslim Brotherhood had not yet been elected, but his pious party members reckoned they had a good chance. Someone was always demonstrating somewhere in the city.

When I told Raif on the telephone about the demonstrations, he was very interested. He wanted to know exactly how many people had gathered, whose side they were on, how the police had behaved and what the overall atmosphere was like. Often I wasn't able to give him precise answers. I was able to tell him with certainty that it was unwise for a woman to approach those assemblies on her own, because the papers were full of horror stories: "There have been several attacks on women," I told him. "They even assaulted a western journalist."

Raif was shocked by the violence that accompanied the revolution. "The Egyptians are experiencing a historically important moment—and some of them are behaving like animals," he said furiously.

After about two weeks I found a flat for us through one of the many agencies in the city. It was in the district of Medinat El-Rehab, quite far out, near the airport. The three rooms were not particularly beautiful, in accordance with our purse, but at least they were furnished.

Our host bade us farewell with some kind words. "You're leaving us already, madame? What a shame!" he dissembled. "My wife and I had just got used to you and your charming children." But I knew that in reality he was relieved: for a man in his position it was anything but politic to host the family of a critic of the regime. The eyes and ears of the Saudi state are everywhere, even in Egypt.

I scrubbed the flat like a wild thing. But I had a feeling that I couldn't get it quite clean: the furniture was old and worn, the beds saggy. I found myself repelled by it and I felt like a stranger. At last I went out with the children to buy new bedclothes and pillows. That way we could at least make our new home look a little nicer.

The next problem was the Internet connection: there wasn't one. I asked the state telephone company what I had to do to get a wireless connection. They laughed long and loud. "Wireless? In your part of town all we can do is offer you a modem. With medium speed. And that will take between six and eight weeks."

"For heaven's sake!" I exclaimed. What sort of developing country had I ended up in? I couldn't wait as long as that: the Internet was my connection with Raif; we phoned and chatted via various servers like Skype or Tango. I needed access straightaway. And I wanted to go on following Raif's blog.

Now I was able to use my experiences during our early days in Jeddah when, with no family and having difficulties in our marriage, I was able to independently make contact with other women. So in desperation I rang the doorbell of the woman who lived above me and asked her if she had an Internet connection. "Yes," she said—and said I could use it whenever I wanted. She was called Hamideh; a plump woman in her mid-thirties, she was very nice. She offered me tea and we chatted for a while. I told her that Raif was still in Jeddah. For professional reasons. I had the feeling that she welcomed the exchange. Suddenly she had an idea: "We could lay a cable from my flat to yours."

"A cable?" I thought for a moment. Of course! It was a

brilliant idea. If I had access to her modem plug, I could dial up the Net at any time. "That would be fantastic!"

Hamideh was immediately consumed with enthusiasm for her idea. Of course I offered to help to pay for the connection. In an electronics shop I bought an extension cable and we laid it along the staircase from her flat to mine. It fitted perfectly through the crack under the door.

"Do you think your husband will be happy with that?" I asked her as we admired our day's work.

"I'll explain it to him," she assured me. "After all, you are a guest in our country. It's my duty to help you."

After that I often did things with Hamideh. She had a twelve-year-old son and no other children. So she was a bit bored at home. Often she came with me and my gang of rascals on a walk to the playground. Then we would sit down in a café and have a Coca-Cola, while the children romped around outside. It was much more interesting than sitting there all on my own.

Once we went off to fulfill Dodi's long-cherished desire to see the Pyramids. They are a few miles from the center of Cairo, southwest of the district of Giza. We went there together on the underground, then took a taxi — and engaged one of the many tour guides who announced their services outside the area. Because of the revolutionary unrest there were hardly any tourists around. The prices were at rock bottom and we had free choice.

The Egyptian took us to the Pharaoh's monument, which cast long shadows in the late afternoon sun, and we entered the pyramid from the northern side. As we followed him down the long, low passageways into the interior, the children listened excitedly to his stories about Cheops, who had ruled this country on the Nile more than 4,500 years ago. In the queen's chamber, a cool stone vault, he told them that the organs of Cheops' mother, who had, like her son, been mummified, were stored separately from her body in a special container. I saw how grimly thrilled the children were by those ideas.

Then we entered the king's burial chamber with the big granite sarcophagus. Dodi immediately ran over to it. But to his great disappointment he discovered that the stone tomb was open and empty. "Where's the mummy?" he asked our guide.

"It's disappeared," said the Egyptian.

"Why?" asked Dodi. "Didn't it like the visitors?"

"That could be," the man said. "When mummies feel oppressed they run away and hide somewhere else among the stones to have a bit of peace."

Dodi nodded sympathetically. "We should probably come back at night, when there's less going on," he reflected — and looked around to check that he couldn't find a trace of Cheops somewhere. "Can we do that, Mum?"

"Let's see."

"Perhaps with Dad!" He tugged pleadingly on my sleeve. "Oh, pleeeease!"

"We'll decide when he's here," I appeased him.

Over time, things with the children got a bit too much. They didn't go to school or kindergarten, so they were hanging around at home all the livelong day. Still, I had taken on a private teacher who gave them a few math and English lessons so that they would pass their exams at the end of the school year. I wanted to wait until the start of the next school year before enrolling them at a regular school: then Raif would be with us, and we could be sure that we were staying.

When I had put them to bed in the evening, often I would sit at the table and read the latest articles on the forum. I was particularly interested in what Raif himself had written. It was an opportunity for me to be close to him, if not physically, then at least intellectually, by sharing in his ideas.

Evening after evening I waited feverishly for that appointment with Raif. I knew that since we had been away he used most of his time to write articles for his blog and for the newspapers. So now, not least because his entrepreneurial activities had flopped, he devoted all his time to writing.

The big subject that engaged him during this time was the Islamist trends which, along with the Arab Spring, were gaining ground in more and more countries — in Syria and Libya above all, but also in Egypt. "A lot of pious Islamic activists in our region dream of a reintroduction of the caliphate," he wrote in an article published in February in *al-Hewar al Mutamaddin*. "There is a systematic mass-mobilization under way, in which ordinary citizens are indoctrinated by being constantly exposed to religion and religiosity."

Sometimes I became uneasy when I read things like that. By writing such words, was Raif putting himself in even greater danger than he was in already? On the other hand I knew that he had no option but to keep on writing. It was his internal commission. Even though he felt the air around him getting thinner, he had to do it.

There was still no sign of Raif joining us. When I asked him if he had done anything about getting his full civil rights back, he used to say to me regularly, "No. But I'll sort things out over the next few days. I'll go to the legal authorities and say to them, 'So, here I am! Tell me what you want of me!' "

"Fine," I told him. But over time I gradually stopped believing that he was really going to do it. Raif was scared of taking that step — because he wasn't sure of the consequences.

"What's the worst that can happen?" I asked him. "They can't just lock you up, can they?"

I didn't like his thoughtful silence.

"Well you'll have to do something. We can't stay in this state forever."

"I know, I know, Ensaf," he said, exhausted.

"We're running out of money."

"Trust me, I'll sort things out. Just be a bit patient with me."

I don't think Raif really had a plan. His supreme goal had been to get me and the children to safety. For himself, he had no strategy. He shied away from confrontation, fearing — rightly — that his battle against the regime would not be a fair dispute among equal partners.

"If you don't come, we'll just come back," I threatened.

"Ensaf, no!" There was a hint of panic in his voice. "I'll go."

"Don't forget to put the children down for their exams. They're in three weeks."

"Do they really have to do those exams?"

"Of course. If you don't come, we'll all come back. And then they'll have to go back to school."

Raif thought for a moment. "I'd rather you stayed," he said.

"But the children need their father! They're always asking after you!" That was the truth: Najwa, Dodi and Miriam couldn't understand why their father was always working, when he had promised them several times that he would join us. They started demanding more and more heatedly that he keep his promise. I knew that I was touching a sore spot with Raif when I told him that. He missed his children very much. "And I'd like to see my husband again!"

It went back and forth like that. In the end he gave in. I convinced Raif that I would come back with the children in early April, even if just to collect him. "That means we're on the safe side where school is concerned," I argued. "If you've sorted everything out by then, we can wind up the flat and go away again. But all together."

Raif agreed, but he wasn't very happy with the decision. In his eyes it involved an unnecessary risk. Unlike me, he had understood long ago that there was no future for us in Saudi Arabia.

But Egypt no longer seemed the ideal place for us either. I had been here twice on holiday, once as a child with my father and once with Raif. I had liked it very much both times. But now I didn't feel quite at ease here. The city of Cairo seemed too big, too noisy, too full, but I didn't feel at home in the country either. Living here was very different from cruising down the Nile on holiday, or exploring the Pyramids. Living here was stressful. Perhaps it was because I was all alone and missed Raif very much.

The political upheavals that were in full swing right then also made me feel uneasy. I stayed away from big gatherings of people when I was with the children. But it was almost impossible to avoid them altogether, because certain squares were always occupied or streets blocked. The devout Muslim Brotherhood, which claimed responsibility on their banners for the fall of Mubarak — even though they had really tended to be onlookers during the revolution — were constantly gaining popularity and influence. More and more women were veiling themselves; it hadn't been like that during my last stay. While I enjoyed finally walking around outside Saudi Arabia in jeans and short-sleeved T-shirt, and of course without a head-covering, they were putting on the orthodox outfit of their own free will. I found that frightening. Could it be that they would soon give this country a religiously inspired government? And if so, how would that government deal with people like Raif? In which direction would Egypt, once a generous, liberal holiday paradise, go over the next few years?

I told Raif on the telephone about my concerns — and he shared them: "If the Muslim Brotherhood become the governing party, it will be a disaster for the country," he said.

The elections in Egypt were set for the end of May 2012. I suggested that Raif should at least wait for their outcome before we made a decision. He agreed. So I prepared everything for our departure: I wound up the flat and packed our two suitcases to fly back to Jeddah. The children too packed their little rucksacks, in which they carried their fluffy animals and any particularly precious toys. Because of course they were needed as hand luggage. I myself was so excited about seeing Raif, about living with him again, that for a while I simply repressed the difficulties that awaited us in Saudi Arabia.

Shortly before takeoff I received a call on my phone. "Are you Mrs. Ensaf Haidar?" a man's voice asked.

"Yes," I replied uncertainly.

"I've already spoken to your husband," said the man, who introduced himself as a friend of Raif's. He too is an affluent and very influential person in Saudi Arabia, which is why, for security reasons, I'll just call him Faris. It means "knight" in Arabic. "I would like to invite you to come to Lebanon," he said. "I would pay for your tickets from Cairo to Beirut, as well as for a six-month stay."

"And Raif knows about that?"

"Yes. He thinks it's a good idea."

I didn't know what to say. Had Raif orchestrated this so that I wouldn't come back to Saudi Arabia? Was the situation that tense? Perhaps he hadn't been able to talk about it on the telephone.

"Many thanks for your offer," I said to Mr. Faris. "That's extraordinarily kind and very generous of you, but first I'll have to talk to my husband about it."

"Of course," he replied. "I'm at your disposal at any time."

As soon as he had hung up I called Raif and took him to task: "What's going on?" I asked him. "Don't you want us to come?"

"Of course I would like you to come, Ensaf," he said, distressed. "I think of nothing but you and the children; I live for you. But the situation here hasn't..." he struggled to find the words, "... hasn't got any better."

"What are you saying I should do?"

"You're free to decide."

"OK," I said. "I'll go to Lebanon with the children if you think that's the right thing. Fine." I took a deep breath. "But first we're coming to Jeddah, to see you!" I knew my decision might not have been the most intelligent, but after four months of separation I just had to see Raif. That was my one condition.

When I boarded the plane in Cairo, I got terrible jitters. I had never liked Jeddah particularly. Still, I yearned for the city that had become home to Raif and me.

Raif was already standing in the arrivals hall waiting for us when we arrived. The children ran toward him. Raif hugged all three of them at the same time. For a long time he just held them and smiled. He looked very, very happy. But I was startled when I saw that while we were away he had got his first gray hairs. They ran like silver threads through his thick hair, which had formerly been pitch black. He looked exhausted, and seemed to have aged several years.

"My beloved Ensaf," Raif greeted me tenderly. "Thank you for having your way. Thank you for letting me see you all."

I looked at him and understood that he saw the time that I had negotiated for us with my stubbornness as a gift. A gift that he wouldn't have allowed himself. This week in Jeddah, our last week with Raif in ages, was one of the loveliest in our life together.

Even today I am glad that I forced him to do it. Einstein was right: in retrospect it doesn't matter in the slightest whether we spent a week, a month or a year together. Time was relative, it stretched. The only important thing was that we spent it together. Those precious moments have branded themselves for ever on my heart.

I found our flat in an impeccable state. Raif, who had put a mattress down in the sitting room while we were away and hadn't used the other rooms at all, had launched a big cleaning operation before we arrived. He wanted everything to be exactly as we had left it, so that the children didn't feel strange there either. And he succeeded: he had even made the beds.

On each bed there lay presents for the bed's occupant: that is Raif's usual way of giving presents. On our marital bed I found two dresses: a summer dress with a colorful pattern of flowers and a tight, shoulderless dress in red silk. Sexy, the way we both like it. He also gave me a skirt with a snakeskin pattern, again in red. I immediately packed all three items in my suitcase. Today they hang in my wardrobe in Canada. When I see them I have to smile with amusement — and at the same time I become nostalgic. Unfortunately in Canada people don't wear such risqué outfits.

I had taken on a difficult task for my time in Jeddah: I wanted to wind up our flat and sell the furniture. If we no longer had a future in Saudi Arabia, then it was the right step. But at the same time it was a very painful one. It didn't feel good bringing one's old life to a close before one had a new life — indeed, not even a vague idea what that life would be — within range. All we knew was that the children and I would go to Lebanon and wait for Raif there. But when he would come was just as much in the stars as the question of what we would do next: where we would stay and what we would live on. Only one thing was clear. The old model wasn't working anymore; it had to go. And we needed a new model — any model.

Most of our things I simply gave away: a friend got the big sitting-room rug, a neighbor the deep freeze that I had only bought six months before. When I started giving away the children's toys I encountered furious resistance. All three refused to give away their treasures. I had put Miriam's Barbie in the handbag of a friend with a daughter of a similar age and Miriam, who was five at the time, simply went and got it back. "No, Mum," she hissed at me. "That's my Barbie!"

I promised her that her father would buy her a new and much nicer doll when we moved into our new house in Lebanon.

She looked at me as if she didn't believe me any more. "When's that going to happen?" she asked suspiciously. She had already waited in vain for her father to arrive in Egypt.

Raif spent almost all his time with the children. He was very concerned that he wouldn't see them for a long time. Most of the time he looked very oppressed and thoughtful. I almost want to say he was depressed. Perhaps it was because he was now at home on his own for long hours. I think that writing while we were away was the only thing that kept him alive. But he also knew that he was taking a lot of risks. He felt that something was heading his way. And he was scared of it. But if you don't know exactly what you're scared of you can't fight your fear: it put Raif in a kind of paralysis. He was hesitant about everything he did, for fear of doing something wrong.

He himself no longer seemed to believe that he could get his travel ban lifted in the foreseeable future. Of course he didn't say that quite so directly. Not to me — and certainly not to the children. But I clearly felt that he had lost his confidence. "If you can't get out legally, you may have to try illegal means," I said to him. "Perhaps you can travel out via Yemen." I had heard that lots of refugees from Africa took that route to get to Saudi Arabia. Perhaps with the right contacts you could travel the other way too? But Raif wouldn't hear of such foolhardy plans.

"I'm a citizen of this country," he said. "Why should I put myself in the hands of people traffickers to leave my homeland?" With such words he tried to deny the oppressive reality, the increasing hopelessness of his situation. He didn't want to give me and the children any sign of his concern. By day he played with them a lot. At night when they were asleep he crept into their room and watched them, sometimes for hours at a time.

We took a lot of photographs that week. I can still see Raif sitting with all three children on the lawn in a friend's garden, hugging them tightly. Or posing with his daughters: Miriam in a princess dress with a crown, Najwa cuddled gently against his shoulder. Once he photographed them when, exhausted, they fell asleep on the floor of the nursery after playing. We still couldn't have guessed that these souvenirs were all we would be left with.

On the day of their end-of-year exams he drove Najwa and Dodi to school in the car. They attended the same school, which taught girls and boys in separate buildings. Najwa had to wear a hijab even as a nine-year-old. Raif encouraged her to do her best. "Show your teachers that there's more under your headscarf than the beautiful long hair they're so scared of," he said to her. "Show them there's a clever brain under there." He waited in his car until they both came back.

"That was really easy. I think I'll do very well," Najwa announced proudly. Dodi was just as pleased.

But the results of the exams wouldn't be announced for another few weeks. We didn't have that much time. Even today we don't know how well Najwa and Dodi did.

I would have loved to extend our stay in Jeddah. I wanted to spend more time with Raif. Only one more week, only one day. But he pleaded with me to leave quickly. "As much as I like lying next to you at night, Ensaf, I'll sleep better when the four of you are in Lebanon," he said to me. "Anything could happen here, any day."

He didn't specify what it might be. And I didn't ask any more questions. I was sick with worry: how much longer was

I supposed to torture my brain over something that couldn't be understood? I think Raif deliberately didn't tell me everything because he was afraid that I would refuse to go. He only gave hints. "This fatwa has no legal value. Even if it's what my father would want. It's just a religious opinion, not a legal one," he said for example, as if to bolster us both up. But I didn't believe his rationalizations and reassurances. His words showed me that he was still unsettled by the fatwa, and that he had bad feelings about what might happen, in spite of his protestations to the contrary.

So after a week I packed our suitcases. As I was sure this time that we wouldn't be coming back, I also took along two old photograph albums. Otherwise I put in a pair of trousers, a jacket and some shirts for Raif. I knew he had been invited to "Liberals' Day" in Lebanon, which was to be held the following month. Raif felt that this was a distinction, and was very keen to take part. "Maybe I'll manage to get there," he said, trying to lift my hopes. "Then I'll need a few decent clothes to wear."

In the sitting room, when we left it, there was only a mattress and a television set. Raif promised me he would take care of everything else. We got to the airport at about five o'clock in the evening, and bought sandwiches because we hadn't eaten anything all day. We ate them together on the benches in the waiting area. Those were our last precious minutes together.

In contrast to our first departure for Egypt, this time we didn't manage to create a good mood and play down our anxiety. The children were clearly aware that something was wrong. No one talked about holidays. We were leaving Jeddah, never to come back: that much was clear even to them. Even though they didn't yet understand why we were taking such a step.

When the time to say goodbye had come, I really had to pull myself together. It was as if a stopwatch was running. Raif hugged and kissed the children, while I watched as if paralyzed.

"Promise me you'll be nice to your mother?" Raif said to the children.

They nodded eagerly — and giggled guiltily.

"You all have to do what she tells you, you hear that?"

"Yes, we promise, Dad," said Dodi, who clearly felt he was being specifically addressed. "We won't annoy her."

I missed out on the hugs, because as always I was hidden under my black cloth. Only a fleeting kiss from Raif brushed my niqab at forehead level — and his smell: Raif's beloved smell, mixed with a hint of Chanel Bleu. I greedily inhaled it as if I would never have the opportunity again.

Those last moments with Raif have etched themselves into my memory. Even today I can see him standing in front of me, with his pale face and his hair run through with fine gray threads, in the dark trousers and white shirt that he was wearing that day. His eyes sad, helpless, full of dark premonitions of what was to come. Not a trace of a smile on his lips.

This was the man I had married ten years before. The man I loved, and would love for all eternity. How had we ended up in that tragic situation? How would we escape it? When would I ever see him again?

"Now go," urged Raif, who like me was struggling to maintain his composure. He didn't want to start crying in front of the children.

"See you soon, don't be long!" I called to him, pushing the little ones in front of me to escape the situation as quickly as possible.

"Take care. I love you!" he called after us. Then he turned around and hurried away.

# CHAPTER SIX

# OUR WORLD COLLAPSES

We got to Beirut at night, and took a taxi into the city center. Raif's friend had reserved a hotel room there in the Christian district, right next to the mile-long promenade and shopping street of the Corniche.

The next day I went exploring for the first time with the children. Beirut was quite different from Cairo. You could see that at first sight. Because of its coastal situation and French influence the city looks less oriental and more Mediterranean. The Christian district at least looks quite modern.

I nostalgically remembered the honeymoon that Raif and I had spent here. In those days the city had been more or less intact. The summer war with Israel five years ago had demolished numerous buildings, particularly in the Shi'ite south of Beirut. But the Lebanese, who were used to destruction and reconstruction since the civil war, had quickly got their city up and running again. The flow of large amounts of foreign capital into the country — not least from Saudi Arabia — had accelerated the reconstruction of the demolished buildings.

As I had done in Egypt, I took on an agency to find a flat

for us. I imagined a safer and more peaceful environment for the children. An environment in which there were no political or religious disputes and where I could let them play in the street in the afternoon without worrying. I knew there was such a neighborhood here. During our honeymoon Raif and I had seen it: the little Christian villages that lay idyllically in the Lebanese mountains north of Beirut. With their European architecture, moderate climate and opulent greenery you almost felt you were in France, I thought. A lot of French was spoken in the schools too. The war between Israel and Hezbollah seemed to have bypassed this part of the country completely. It was there and nowhere else that I wanted to live with the children.

After some searching the agency found a flat that matched my ideals. It was in Brumana, a mountain village half an hour from Beirut. It was in a very picturesque situation, surrounded by green hills, with groves of firs and pines which had a sweet, resinous smell in the summer. At the weekend hordes of tourists came there from the capital, because it was so beautiful. For the sake of caution I didn't tell the Saudi embassy, which had automatically been informed about our place of residence in Lebanon, that we were changing address.

Our flat wasn't very big, but it was cozy and clean. It had two bedrooms. I furnished one for the children; in the other there was a big double bed. That was where Raif and I would sleep. I particularly liked the big balcony that led off that room. The sun shone on it in the morning, and I made it a habit to drink my coffee there or smoke a cigarette.

I enrolled the children in a Catholic private school: Najwa in the third year and Dodi for the second. Miriam would go to preschool. I organized a private teacher for them, who came twice a week to give them French lessons, because at school they would be taught in that language. Of course it would be hard for them at first. But they had the whole of the summer holidays to get to know the language—and I was convinced that they would profit from it in the long run.

I myself hoped to make friends in the idyllic little village more quickly than I might have done in the big anonymous city of Beirut. That also proved to be the case. The neighbors, most of them Christians, were open and friendly toward me. And when I went to a playground with the children I quickly fell into conversation with the other mothers. These were hopeful beginnings for later friendships. I was quite pleased by how well I had organized our life in such a relatively short time. Now all we needed was Raif to turn up; then everything would be perfect, I thought.

One evening in the middle of April, when I had already put the children to bed, I sat down on my balcony to relax over a can of malt beer and a cigarette. I scanned the news from Saudi Arabia. Our crown prince and, for many years, interior minister Emir Naif, a conservative hard-liner, had died, it said. So he wouldn't be following our old king on to the throne. I wasn't sure who would take his place. Raif was bound to know. What would he think of this news?

Suddenly I missed him even more than usual. How lovely it would be if he were here now too and we could talk about these things together, I thought. I sent him a message via WhatsApp. Nothing political. "How are you, my darling?"

He didn't reply.

"I miss you. Have you had a nice day?"

He didn't reply.

I sent the message again. "I miss you. Have you had a nice day?"

Nothing.

Obviously he wasn't online, as my messages were marked unread. All right then, perhaps not; he would probably call later on. As the beer had made me dozy, I decided to go to bed unusually early. I lay down on the bed and went straight to sleep.

The next morning I reached for my phone. Now that Raif and I were forcibly separated from one another, we were behaving as we had done at the start of our relationship: we constantly wrote each other messages. We sent chats or spoke on the phone, so that in spite of the distance he participated very intensely in my life and that of the children. In Lebanon it was no different from what we'd done a few months ago in Egypt. When I woke up, I was usually greeted by one of his little hearts, sent to my phone during the night.

This morning, however, I didn't find a single heart, and no missed calls. Normally Raif spent the whole night bombarding me with messages, because he often slept badly. But today he hadn't even read the two short communications that I had sent him the previous evening. The system told me as much. It was very, very unusual. I frantically checked the other chat services that we used. Nothing. He clearly hadn't been online at all.

I had an extremely bad feeling, and called his number. I got the ringing tone, but no one answered. I hung up and tried again. Sometimes there was something wrong with the connections. But even after I'd rung several times he didn't pick up.

I stood up, perplexed, and tottered out of bed to brush my

teeth. After that I tried again. Nothing. My unease mounted. What was going on? Could it be that Raif was still asleep? Was he ill? Or had he switched his phone to silent? Had he left or lost it somewhere?

I looked for the number of his second phone, which he used for business contacts, but it was completely switched off. My unease was mixed with helplessness. Something at home in Jeddah was going wrong—and from here there was nothing I could do. I tried the number again and again. Eventually he *had* to pick up, I thought. It was incredibly disturbing.

By now the children had woken up too. They skipped into my bed and tried to start a pillow fight, their favorite occupation. But I didn't feel like having fun today. I brusquely shooed them into the bathroom and told them to brush their teeth and get dressed. As usual Miriam took an eternity to choose her outfit, and I noticed that I didn't have that much patience with her today.

I set a bowl of cornflakes down on the kitchen table in front of each of them. I wasn't hungry. While they were busy with breakfast, I went out on to the balcony and dialed Raif's number again. When he still didn't pick up, I called Turad. He always knew where Raif was.

"Hi, Turad," I said. "I haven't been able to get through to Raif since last night."

Turad was very surprised to have me on the line.

"I last saw him yesterday afternoon," he said, sounding slightly puzzled. He promised to drive to our flat and see what was up. "Don't worry, madame," he said. "I'll tell you as soon as I know anything."

"Thank you," I murmured, and dialed Raif's number again.

I don't know how often I tried that morning. Twenty times? Fifty times? Countless times. After a while I kept pressing the redial button out of simple despair: I had no idea what else to do.

At about the fifty-second attempt someone suddenly answered. I was almost speechless with surprise when I heard a deep man's voice at the other end. But it wasn't Raif's voice.

"Who the hell is this?" it asked angrily. "You're getting on our nerves!"

I gave a terrible start. "Where is my husband?" I asked shrilly.

"He's in jail."

And before I could ask him another question the stranger simply hung up.

I had to sit down. So it had happened. The very thing we had always been afraid of: Raif had been arrested. But why? What exactly had happened? And what was he being accused of?

The man who had Raif's telephone would certainly be able to answer those questions. When I had come to myself a little, I pressed the redial button again. I needed to find out more. But the man didn't pick up. I tried again and again: in vain. No one answered.

For a while I sat there, perplexed, on my folding chair on the balcony and stared into the void. The children were rampaging noisily about their room. Miriam came out crying and said that the other two were annoying her. By way of proof she let a few tears spill out from under her pink glasses. But I couldn't get involved. "Please sort it out among yourselves," I said, and sent her back to her brother and sister.

I had to think. What could I do? Who might know any-thing? I called one of Raif's liberal friends, a writer he met often. "That's impossible!" he said in surprise. "Raif was at my house yesterday." He too promised to make some inquiries and then call me back.

Next I called Walid Abu al-Khair, Raif's brother-in-law. He sounded rather alarmed when I told him about my brief exchange with the man who had answered Raif's phone. "Can you please investigate what's going on?" I asked him. I hoped that because he was a lawyer he might be able to approach the authorities and find out more.

"Of course, Ensaf."

After half an hour Walid called me back. "Yes, it's true," he said. "Raif's being held in investigative custody." He didn't know anything more than that: either what Raif was being accused of, or how long he would stay in jail. "Don't worry about it," he said, though, trying to reassure me. "I'm sure it'll all be fine. I'll have him out in a few days." Walid promised me he would take care of everything. "I'll make sure he's all right."

"OK. Thanks, Walid," I said a little more calmly.

I was finding it very difficult to deal with the situation. Uncertainty is a terrible state: I didn't want to think neg-atively, in order to avoid getting myself down. But I didn't want to think too positively either, because I was afraid of disappointment. So I tried not to think at all, which of course didn't work.

For the next few hours I did nothing but phone Raif's friends. Since they include some influential people, as I have said, I hoped that one of them might know more. It was only after lengthy investigations that I managed to discover exactly what had happened on the evening when he had disappeared.

It must have gone a bit like this: in the evening Raif had realized that he was hungry. His love of fast food had led him in the direction of the nearest McDonald's drive-in. On the way he was stopped at a road check. The officers demanded to see his driving license. Raif produced the document. But it had run out: as the authorities had denied his existence for a long time, he had had no chance of renewing it. So he was driving without a legal license. That was why the police had taken him to the station. There they checked his identity — and when they discovered who they were dealing with they thought it would be a good idea to inform their superiors. So Raif ended up in investigative custody — although at first without any specific charges. His opponents were probably still trying to come up with something to charge him with.

After two weeks I finally got a call from him. I almost jumped when he was suddenly on the line in person. I quickly went out on to the balcony with the phone so that the children couldn't hear us.

"I'm in investigative custody, I'm fine," he said. Of course I didn't believe that for a second. He probably had to say that because a security man was standing beside him.

"Just imagine: I'm locked up in a cell with criminals," he told me, apparently amused. I was struck less by his remark than by his fake cheerfulness. But I tried to compose myself. I wanted to show him that I was strong. I wanted to give him strength. And he clearly wanted to do the same. "We'll soon sort out this misunderstanding," he said. "Don't worry about it."

"When will they let you out?" I asked excitedly.

"Walid's working on it."

Then the man standing next to him reminded Raif that his time on the telephone had run out. We had talked to each other for exactly two minutes. "Don't tell the children anything about this," he added.

"No. Absolutely not."

For the first few weeks after Raif's arrest my patience was put sorely to the test. For a long time no one knew what accusations would be leveled against him, or for how long he would have to stay in jail. Even Walid, who was now officially representing him as his lawyer, couldn't tell me. I was in a state of complete uncertainty. The children often asked me why their father, who had called every five minutes before, had suddenly stopped ringing. I had no answer. During that time I very rarely had a chance to talk to him in person.

Every time my phone vibrated and I saw an unfamiliar number on the display, I flinched inwardly. Was this going to be good news — or more bad tidings? Instinctively I always fled on to the balcony before I answered. I was bracing myself for anything.

"Are you Ensaf Haidar, the wife of Mr. Raif Badawi?" asked the caller who rang me one morning in early May 2012.

"Yes, why?" I had got used to being suspicious.

The man introduced himself as Anwar Rashed, a liberal activist. He was also a friend of Faris, our patron. "Mr. Faris would like to send a car to your flat," he informed me. "Liberals' Day is being held at the Gulf Forum in Beirut today — and your husband is going to be honored. It would be an honor for us if you would accept the prize on his behalf."

That was the last thing I had expected. Raif had mentioned this "Liberals' Day," but not that he was supposed to be receiving a prize at it. And in all the hubbub about his arrest I had completely forgotten the date. In comparison with the horrific news that I had been receiving over the past few weeks, this was something good: I too took it as an honor that Raif was to be given such an award. Perhaps that acknowledgment would even help him in his dispute with the authorities.

"I'd love to come," I said immediately.

"Fabulous," said the man. "The car will be there in two hours."

I feverishly wondered what to wear. I wanted to seem serious, but on the other hand not too stiff. So I opted for a combination: I wore jeans, a green blazer and a colorful silk neck-scarf. I smartened up the children as well: if their father was being honored, they should definitely come with me and be present at the ceremony.

As we drove toward Beirut in the limousine, I felt increasingly agitated. What on earth was I going to say? I had no experience of these matters. I was just incredibly proud of my husband, who didn't yet know anything about the award that he was about to be given.

When I entered the hall with the 150 participants, I felt very queasy indeed. The children sat down in the audience; Dodi had his camera at the ready. I waited until the organizer gave me a sign. Then I went up onstage. He gave me a gilded plaque: "The Gulf Forum for Civil Societies is awarding this prize to the liberal human rights activist Mr. Raif Badawi in acknowledgment of his views and his liberal activities," was the dedication engraved on it.

The presenter handed me the microphone — and my heart thumped in my throat. Of course I had been brooding about what I should say. "Many thanks." My voice broke when I tried to speak. I tried to calm myself down. "This award gives us a great boost. A boost that Raif and I can really use."

The audience applauded. I didn't say anything more. I couldn't, because I didn't want to babble in front of the children. I was pleased to see Dodi eagerly snapping away in the audience. Yes, let him be proud of his father. I didn't want to trouble him with anything else.

We spent another lovely day in Beirut. Souad, the co-founder of Raif's network, had come as well. She invited us to a fish restaurant. "We're all there for you," she said to me. "If you need anything, if we can help in any way, just tell us." I thanked her from the bottom of my heart. It's so important to have friends.

In the evening I had the chance to speak to Raif on the phone. "You've won a prize," I told him, radiant with joy — and then gave him an account of our day in Beirut, and how I had accepted the prize on his behalf. And that all his friends sent him greetings.

Raif was very proud, I could tell. The children were allowed to talk to him briefly. "I took a lot of photographs for you," Dodi told him. "When are you coming, Dad?"

"Soon," he lied. "Very soon."

I spoke often to Walid on the phone. He kept me abreast of how Raif's case was developing. But he gave me the information in small and digestible doses. "Don't fret, Ensaf," he would say. "Raif will soon be with you again." His optimism made me underestimate the scale of the problem for a long time — and even made me impatient. How long would it go on, I wondered after a few weeks: when would Walid finally get Raif out? After all, he had only been caught with an expired driving license! It was not until later that I would discover he had kept a few things from me in his account of what had happened.

I realized that more precisely on the day when I suddenly couldn't get hold of Walid. I knew that on that day Raif was supposed to appear before the court. They picked him up from investigative custody at seven o'clock in the morning. In the afternoon I tried to get through to Walid to find out how the session had gone. But he didn't answer my calls.

I was furious. What was going on? As Raif's wife I had a right to learn where I stood.

At last Raif himself called. He sounded depressed. He gave me a very detailed account of his session with the judge Abdul-Rahman al-Jarbu.

"He told me I should apologize to the Almighty and do penance."

"What for?"

"For my supposed loss of faith. He said: 'Say three times the Muslim confession of faith: There is no God but Allah, and I testify that Mohammed is his prophet.'"

"And did you do that?"

"No." Raif had refused, as he sensed a trap. If he uttered the formula for conversion to Islam, that could be treated as proof that he had previously lost his faith—and thus as a confession of guilt. "That isn't necessary, as I am already a Muslim," he had said to the judge. "Say it yourself. Why me?"

Raif told me the course of the discussions down to the tiniest minutiae. At the very end he said very calmly, at peace with himself: "Can you imagine that, Ensaf? When the judge said I deserved the death sentence I thought of you and smiled. I had your image in front of my eyes—and you brought me joy."

That was the moment when my world, as I had previously known and loved it, broke down once and for all. My back slid slowly down the wall of the house until I was sitting on the floor of the balcony. When I opened my mouth to gasp for air and give Raif an answer, a scream of despair forced its way out from my very depths.

I was sick for a week. The children were very worried, as I was barely able to get out of bed and supply them with the things they needed. It was as if someone had severed my lifeline: I couldn't go on. The news that my husband had been accused of apostasy and could expect the death sentence was too much.

Raif called me several times and tried to reassure me. "But Ensaf," he said, "it's only the first accusation. We can respond to it. We'll fight that appraisal!"

He struggled to sound optimistic and give me courage. But I found it hard to take from him. Because Raif was sending me contradictory signals. On the one hand he claimed that everything would be fine. On the other he begged me to apply to the United Nations, as quickly as possible, for political asylum. If anything happened to him, he argued, we would have to travel to a different country. Lebanon would be too unsafe for us, as the Saudi influence is very strong here too. Then we would need the status of political refugees.

"I'm not going anywhere without you, Raif," I said to him.

"And nor should you. It's only a precautionary measure, just in case."

"Be quiet," I cut in. I hated hints like that.

"Fine. You just wait for me — and as soon as I'm free we'll go somewhere together. Perhaps France or Malaysia. What do you think? You'd love it there."

After such conversations I was pulled back and forth between hope and fear. Walid adopted a similar tone when he reemerged from his contemplation. "I'm very sorry, Ensaf," he said at our first phone call. "But there isn't yet anything definitive." He promised me to defend Raif with all his strength. "You really don't need to be scared," he claimed. "Raif isn't an apostate. We all know that, and the judges will know it too. Trust me. I'll get him out of there."

Even Raif's sister Samar, unusually, wanted to talk to me. "Walid will see to it," she tried to comfort me. "He has a lot of experience of such things."

I wanted to believe it. I tried to believe it. But I was still scared. Terribly scared. I woke up screaming at night, and fell silent during the day, because I couldn't let on to the children. That was the most difficult thing: making sure they didn't see what was going on. I didn't want to burden them with it. On the other hand the children helped me too. Because without them I would have had no reason to pull myself together. But life had to go on. Normal family life had to keep going, even though I felt terrible. I had to be strong for them.

So somehow I was trying to return to normality — in spite of the terrible accusations. I had a lot of support from Raif's friends and admirers, who suddenly called me and gave me words of solidarity, or left me messages on Facebook. That felt good. It told me that we weren't entirely alone.

Even people I didn't really know offered me their help. Now that Raif was in jail, and we had no idea when he would be let out again — or whether he would be released at all — I was also worried about our finances. Our rent was 850 dollars a month; school and private lessons for the children weren't cheap either. As a result the money that Faris had given us for the first little while was about to run out. And of course I didn't want to ask for more.

But luckily there were several people like Faisal or Faris in our circle of acquaintances, who very discreetly offered us their help whenever things got tight. That was what Raif's friends were like: they stood by us even in bad times, as they had promised to do. And it meant we could get by.

Of course I also wondered how I could earn some extra money myself. But my possibilities were limited, not just because I had to look after three little children: I became painfully aware that I had no professional training, let alone practical experience in the world of work. Who should I apply to?

The wife of our patron's driver was another great support. She also lived in Brumana and she would often offer me a glass of tea or come with me when I went for a walk. Near my flat, a little further from the center, there were parks, where we sometimes strolled together when the children were at school. Then I would tell her about the latest developments — and she reacted very sympathetically, like a sister. Those walks we took together in the outdoors were incredibly reassuring to me: when I breathed in the resinous scent of the pines here in the peace of the mountains, all the things that we human beings do to each other struck me as completely surreal.

But unfortunately I also experienced the opposite: people close to me turned away because they didn't want to have anything to do with the wife of an apostate. Or they recommended that I distance myself from Raif. The worst disappointment in that respect was my family. After the great row between them and Raif at the start of our marriage I could hardly believe that things could get worse. But I was to be mistaken. Rather than standing by me in that difficult situation, as I would have wished, they brought me many more problems and worries.

I had already known that there was something wrong when we were living in Jeddah. After we moved away from Jizan, I still had sporadic contact with my parents and my brothers and sisters. But every now and again, on special occasions, I went home. Once I visited them because my father was in poor health. I think it must have been in about 2010. He had just discovered that he had to take a course of dialysis because of his kidney problems. So I boarded a south-bound plane. On my own. Raif avoided my parents' house, as he had been badly treated there and still felt hurt.

The trouble began as soon as I appeared at the door. "Why are you traveling alone?" my brother criticized me. "It's not done. If you had told us, we would have sent someone to accompany you, if your husband can't do it."

They caused a terrible fuss and didn't even want to let me into the house because my behavior had been so unacceptable. It was their old accusation against Raif: that he didn't keep me, his wife, under tight enough control, that he gave me too much freedom. In terms of my clothes, for example: I never wore gloves or an extra veil to cover my eyes. Raif thought it was nonsense. In comparison with them, then, we led a rather unorthodox life. And they were foxed by the fact that we were also such a happy couple. "You're sullying our reputation," my brothers said. "If you try to come into our house we'll beat you."

Yes, they really said that. I begged them at least to be allowed to spend a few hours with my father. We reached an agreement in the end, and they allowed me to visit his sickbed. Afterward, in the late afternoon, I set off for the last flight to Jeddah. Unfortunately I wasn't welcome as a surprise guest. Not even my mother — presumably for fear of my brothers — had made any suggestions in that direction.

On the way to the door my younger brother Adil stopped me. He asked me into the sitting room so that we could have a glass of tea together. I interpreted that as a gesture of reconciliation. But I was mistaken. When we were sitting together on the sofa he said something very curious. "What do you think about getting divorced from Raif?" he suggested.

I was openmouthed with astonishment at this bizarre idea. "Are you crazy? I have three children with him!" I replied furiously.

"You needn't be dependent on him," Adil said. "I'll sort out a villa for you."

"I love Raif," I explained. "I'll never leave him. So you can get that idea out of your head."

Then I left in a hurry. Just get out of this madhouse, I thought to myself. What had got into my brother, to suggest something like that? A divorced woman in Saudi Arabia has anything but laudable status. I thought it was incredible to think that I might be willing to put myself in that position unless I really needed to.

I knew that Adil and the other members of my family didn't like Raif's network — and above all the fact that it had made him so famous. They weren't comfortable with the idea of having "liberals" in the family. Not because they themselves were so pious and God-fearing, not that: it was more that it threatened their reputation in conservative Jizan. They wanted to be respectable citizens and not, for heaven's sake, have political activities attracting attention, even if they were only those of their brother-in-law. Then, when Raif's father started making his embarrassing appearances on state television, they were thoroughly ashamed that their sister should be married to a man whose own father made such hair-raising accusations against him.

When Raif's problems got worse, they threatened me openly: "Leave him, or you won't get your inheritance." It wasn't up to them, but they said it anyway. And by then my father was too weak to contradict them. The weaker he got, the stronger they became.

When Raif's father's smear campaign in the media had reached its peak, my family also started spreading rumors. My cousin Adel, who also lived in Jeddah, told anyone who would listen that Raif and I had been forced to marry in our youth: the religious police had caught us engaging in immoral activities and ordered us to get married on the spot. That made Raif and me laugh long and loud. At the time at least. But in hindsight it doesn't seem so funny anymore: my own family waged almost as hurtful a campaign against me as Raif's father's campaign against his son.

After Raif's arrest it became very serious. In retrospect I was glad that I had yielded to Raif's urgings and left the country before it was too late. If I hadn't, by then my father would have been able to apply for guardianship over me again. And as he was so weak, my brothers would effectively have been given executive power over me. A horrific thought.

But basically it was never about me. It was always about Raif. They wanted to bring him down.

Their mouthpiece was my sister Mariam, with whom I remained in contact. One evening, shortly after Raif was sentenced, she called me. "How are you, Ensaf?" she asked, with concern in her voice.

"OK. I'm trying not to lose hope," I replied and went out on to the balcony, where I lit a cigarette. "Walid says nothing is certain yet."

"That's good." Mariam cleared her throat. I could tell she wanted to say something to me, but didn't dare come out with it.

"How is Father?"

"Not terribly well. This whole business is putting a terrible strain on him."

I was amazed. Had my father developed sympathy or understanding for my husband in his old age?

"Everyone says you've brought shame on our family," said Mariam. "Anwar and Adil are mad as hornets. I'm worried about what they might do if they see you."

The smoke from my cigarette almost stuck in my throat when I heard that. It made me cough. "Oh, really?" I asked her furiously. I knew very well that Mariam had been given the task of passing this message on to me, even if she didn't say it explicitly. I thought, did my family have no other concerns but their damned reputation? Did they really feel the need to burden me with another problem? "It hasn't occurred to any of you to come to my support!"

"Be careful, Ensaf," Mariam warned me. "They're serious."

"Let them be. There's nothing I can do about it."

"You and Raif have caused a scandal."

"We're the victims of a smear campaign. Why can no one see that?"

Mariam didn't reply. She was caught between the two sides. "I worry for you, little sister. Don't let anyone know your address," she advised me.

"Do you think they're going to come here and harm me?"

Mariam was silent for a long time. "I'm not sure."

My sister's words unsettled me. I gave her a fake address in Lebanon so that she could pass it on to my family if anyone asked for it. If my brothers took it into their heads to do something to me they would find themselves on a wild goose chase, I thought.

The threatening phone calls followed. When I had just picked up my children from their private French lesson, my phone rang in the middle of the street. No number came up, but I answered it anyway.

"Hi, Ensaf," said an unfamiliar male voice. "We know where you are. And if we catch you something very unpleasant is going to happen."

I looked frantically around. I had the feeling that the man on the line must be hiding in the bushes somewhere very nearby.

"Just wait. We'll see each other soon."

I hung up.

"Who was that, Mum?" asked Najwa, noticing the shock on my face.

"Oh, nobody," I said. "It must have been a wrong number."

The children exchanged skeptical glances — and I had the feeling that they didn't really believe me. We adults always imagine that we can hide things — particularly the unpleasant ones — from our children. But in fact they pick up everything.

It wouldn't be the only threatening phone call. Often there were men with different voices on the line, threatening to harm me or the children. A few times they even threatened to kill me. I impressed on my children that they must not talk to strangers, and under no circumstances were they to tell anyone their name if they were asked. In school I informed the headmaster that no one apart from myself had permission to pick them up after school. These were makeshift precautionary measures.

I can't say for certain that my brothers were behind these calls. Perhaps they had commissioned someone else to make them. We had enough enemies, after all. But I suspect that my brothers were somehow involved. I think they were trying to soften me up. Again and again they let me know, via my sister, that there was a way out: divorce from Raif. Then family peace would be restored, and I could come back to Saudi Arabia.

Every time Mariam started on the subject, I pretended she had made a particularly good joke. I wanted to make it clear that it was out of the question as far as I was concerned. I wouldn't have dreamed of leaving Raif. Certainly not now that he was in jail. In my view that would have been nothing but betrayal. How could I have gone on living, how could I have looked myself in the eye? He needed me now. And I was standing by him. I loved him not least because of his liberal opinions. How could I deny him?

When my brothers learned that their threats were falling on stony ground, they changed tactics. Behind my back they called a family council. All seven met up at my parents' house to decide what to do with me. My father should have been involved in the discussions too, but his health was too poor.

My mother and my sisters listened, but had no right to speak or make decisions. My brothers arranged everything among themselves.

They met several times and made two sweeping decisions at those meetings. The first concerned me. My brothers decided to expel me from the family circle. I don't know precisely why. When Mariam tried to tell me about it, I kept interrupting her and said to her, "Leave me in peace. I'm not interested in any of that." It was a protective reaction, because in fact the news was terribly hurtful to me: all seven brothers agreed that from now on I was no longer their sister — and no longer my parents' daughter.

My mother and sisters didn't protest against the decision. And that was a further disappointment to me: how could the women in our family be so weak? In my mother's case I almost understood: she was afraid of my brothers' rage. Because as soon as my father died, she would be completely dependent on them. That's how she was brought up. But my sisters? They had their own families and lived their own independent lives. So there was nothing my brothers could do to them. Still, they kept their mouths shut; they let it happen. I couldn't understand it.

My brothers officially informed the authorities of my expulsion. And they made one other decision, even more presumptuous than the first. They applied to the court in Jeddah to annul my marriage to Raif. "You're about to be divorced," Mariam told me on the phone. "The process is already under way."

I was speechless when I heard that. What were they thinking of? What gave my family the right to get involved in my private life in such a shameless way? A marriage isn't just a piece of paper that you can tear up when you feel like it. It isn't a magazine subscription that you can cancel.

But in Saudi Arabia everything is possible: my brothers and my father really were able to make me divorce Raif without my permission. What played into their hands was the fact that Raif had officially been prejudged as an apostate. The loss of faith in our country is a killer argument: any judge can see that a wife must be released from her marriage vows under those circumstances. No further explanation is needed.

So in all likelihood I am by now officially divorced in Saudi Arabia. I don't know. I don't care, either. What does it mean? My marriage to Raif was made in the sight of God, not in front of a bunch of sanctimonious jurists. It's for eternity. And no earthly judge has the right to question it.

I told Mariam I wanted to hear no more on the matter. "OK, OK. I just wanted you to know what's going on here," she said, trying to play down the issue. "I'm just worried about you." She sensed how furious I was. I thought the whole thing was somehow embarrassing to her. Still, she and the other women in the family had been too weak to defend me. And I held that against them. It hurt me a lot. Even today I haven't overcome the pain that my mother inflicted on me with her silence: how could she leave me so alone in this situation, when I so urgently needed her support, even if all she could offer was emotional solace? Had she completely forgotten our time together?

During our next conversation Mariam revealed to me that she'd been phoning me in secret. "Please don't tell anyone, or I'll get into trouble," she whispered. Finally I blew my top.

"How much of a coward must you be, not even daring to phone your sister?" I hissed at her. "Stand up for yourself! It's not just you and Hanan, but Egbal and Mother too. You're behaving as if you were completely impotent. It's really shaming."

"Ensaf, listen…" she tried to calm me down. But my blood was boiling now.

"I don't need to have you treat me like this!"

Then I simply put the phone down.

The next time Mariam rang I didn't go to the phone. Later I even changed my number so that no one from home could get hold of me in Lebanon. I didn't want any more negative news from home. I didn't want to be hurt anymore. What I was going through with Raif was enough for me. All of a sudden it was too much. I was at the end of my tether.

I spent a very lonely time, trapped with my worries and the permanent fear for Raif's life, in spite of the support that we were given. Walid supported Raif with his appeal, and kept me regularly informed about the state of things, for which I was very grateful. But my most important goal was to keep the children out of the whole sorry business. I wanted them to have as innocent an upbringing as possible. So I struggled to maintain the illusion of a carefree life for their sake.

Whenever Raif had the opportunity to give us a quick call I brought them to the phone so that they could say a few words to their father. He too put on a façade of normality and asked them about their everyday lives: whether they had found friends in Lebanon, what it was like at school, how they were getting on with their French, how they had spent the day.

They had no idea that he was in handcuffs as he asked these questions, with a prison warder standing by his side.

That he was stuck in a cell with lots of other men, and was awaiting the uncertain outcome of his trial. That he was being humiliated and abused. And thank God they didn't know that his beard had turned almost completely white with grief, as Walid had told me.

They often asked Raif why he hadn't joined us long ago, and why for heaven's sake it was taking him so long to get rid of our flat. Sometimes they scolded him too. They told him to hurry up — and he regularly told them that he was doing his best, and that it definitely wouldn't be long. I think it was very hard for him.

But he asked me not to tell them anything about his problems. Certainly not about the fact that he was in prison. Because everyone knows that criminals go to prison, and Raif didn't want his children to think ill of him under any circumstances. Not least for that reason, we kept everything secret from them.

So as not to get myself and the children down I tried to ignore our problems from day to day, and concentrate on positive things. I was glad that Najwa, Dodi and Miriam were learning French so quickly, and making friends in their new school. They are all very open with people, so they soon had Lebanese friends. For my part, I made friends with their mothers. So soon we had stopped being foreigners. Yes, I must say: apart from our family problems we felt very comfortable in our chosen home of Brumana.

But unfortunately the bad news from Saudi Arabia kept coming. The next shock came in the form of a Facebook post. I happened on it more or less by accident; a cousin of Raif's had shared it. It referred to a YouTube video whose author I was very familiar with: Raif's father had turned media star again. He had clearly made the video only very recently; I opened it with a mixture of curiosity and apprehension.

As soon as I pressed the start button, Abu Raif appeared in the familiar setting of his living room. Clearly he had found no sponsors for his new clip. He was sitting in an armchair, wearing a brown cloak, a checked headdress and a black headband. The one he had whipped Raif with in the past, I assumed. He looked straight into the camera through the thick lenses of his glasses.

He appealed to the king, his emirs and the whole of the Saudi government: "I need your help," he said. "I demand the right to bring up the children Najwa, Dodi and Miriam. I want them to be taken away from their mother and their liberal environment. This environment is not good for them. Instead they should grow up in Muslim surroundings."

When I heard this man speaking the names of my children, shivers of cold went up my spine. So far and no further, you old man, I swore to myself: what was this monster thinking of, threatening my children? Wasn't it enough that he had destroyed his own son's life? And now he wanted to do the same to our children? I wouldn't allow that under any circumstances.

In agitation I told Raif about the video the next time he rang from jail. He was horrified. "Be careful, Ensaf. That man is capable of anything." He didn't need to tell me that: you only had to look at Raif to know what Mohammed Badawi was capable of. He had put his own son in jail, and was prepared to risk the chance of his death. No, much worse than that: he was publicly calling for it. He was working actively to extinguish Raif's life, the life that he himself had created. And this wretch, of all people — entirely in line with Saudi law — was now laying claim to our children!

This time I didn't argue with Raif when he urged me once more to put in an asylum application with the United Nations. It was about our children — and I owed it to them at least to bring them to safety from their grandfather. Even if I might not be able to rescue Raif himself.

So one morning when the children were at school I went to Beirut to visit UN headquarters. That sounds more impressive than it actually is. In fact the building merely consists of a collection of containers. When I arrived, an extraordinary number of people were crowding into the building, all, like me, wanting to apply for asylum. The staff were regulating the crush by issuing numbers. After a few hours' wait I was at last allowed into one of the offices. After I had completed the paperwork I was given an appointment with a Lebanese lawyer, a tall, slim woman with short, dark hair. She was very kind and understood my problems immediately.

We worked together on a file in which she described my case. She sent it on to the governments of various countries. "Now you'll have to be patient for a while," she said to me. "It usually takes a few months before a country declares itself willing to accept you as an asylum seeker."

"Isn't there a way of speeding up the whole process?" I asked her nervously.

"No. Sorry. There's nothing to be done. We'll call you as soon as we know anything."

She gave me a friendly pat on the shoulder and ushered me out with a kind smile.

OK, I said to myself: a few months. We could survive that. And who knows, perhaps Raif would already be with us and we could travel together if the authorities gave us the green light to travel to a different country.

In the meantime Raif's appeal had taken an optimistic turn. In January 2013 the civil court in Jeddah passed his case on to the city criminal court. The explanation for this step was important. Since Raif had not slandered Islam in his articles and blogs, the charge of apostasy could not be sustained. Hence the civil court had no jurisdiction.

That allowed me to breathe for a moment. Walid was hopeful too. "You'll see, Ensaf. Eventually we'll all sit together and laugh about all this nonsense," he said. "Don't let it get you down!"

I tried not to. I really tried to bolster Raif's spirits. And in the end I actually allowed myself a degree of restrained optimism, because I heard from all sides that an appeal would be allowed against the sentence. In fact I even got a little impatient: when would the new judge finally deliver his sentence and release my Raif from his martyrdom?

The time came in July. I had the chance to speak to Raif the evening before. "Tomorrow is the hour of truth," he said to me. "Wish me luck!"

"I wish us both luck. All my thoughts will be with you," I said. "I'm sure it will all go well."

That night I couldn't sleep for excitement. Our fate would be decided the following day, I thought. Either they would recognize my husband's innocence; then, after that whole odyssey, we could finally lead a normal life at last — wherever. Or... I preferred not to think that idea through. But it kept me tossing and turning restlessly in bed. At some point during those endless hours the birds in the garden started singing, and I knew the fateful day had dawned. Was Raif already on the way to the courtroom?

The day felt as long as the night before it, because Raif

didn't call me until the evening. I tried to tell by the sound of his voice whether he had good news or bad. He sounded — what should I say? — cautious.

"How did it go?" I asked anxiously.

"Quite good," he said. "OK."

"Did they lift the sentence?"

"Yes."

I heaved a sigh of relief.

"But they passed a new one: six hundred lashes and seven years in prison."

That came as unexpectedly as if I had just received the first lash personally. They were going to whip Raif? Six hundred times? No flesh and blood human being could endure that. They might just as well have decided to beat him to death.

"But...that's impossible — how can they do that?" I stammered.

"I'm sorry, Ensaf," he said, as if apologizing for what they were doing to him. "I wouldn't have expected it either. Please forgive me. I'm so sorry for you and the children, having to put up with this."

Raif tried to control himself. But he started crying, and I cried too. Would this nightmare never end?

When I spoke to Walid he was equally disappointed. "Believe me, Ensaf, I would never have thought that possible," he said. "But we mustn't give up."

"What do you mean?"

"Well, we've got to take the case to appeal again. We can't just accept it!"

"Yes," I agreed with him. If there was any chance of freeing Raif, we had to use it. Otherwise they would whip him to death.

Raif's reaction was calmer. "Walid is a good lawyer, and I'll follow his recommendations." But I clearly sensed the unease in his voice. "We'll do what he says."

"What are you scared of?" I asked him. "It can't get any worse."

"*Insha'allah.* God willing." He fell thoughtfully silent.

"At least we've got to try!"

"Yes, let's try."

News of Raif's new sentence did not go unheard in the Arab world. Many local broadcasters and newspapers reported on it. An editor from CNN even rang me on my mobile. Walid had probably given him my number. "Would you be able to give us a short interview about your husband's sentence?" the man asked. "We've already interviewed his lawyer, Mr. Abu al-Khair."

When I heard that I immediately agreed and invited him to my house. Of course I assumed that Raif's situation could only be improved if more people learned of the injustice being done to him. The American journalist arrived with his cameraman only a few hours later. I smuggled them both past the children's room into the kitchen so that we could speak freely. At that time I wasn't yet particularly practiced at dealing with the press.

When I told him how difficult it was for us as a family to do without Raif, who had now been in prison for over a year, he seemed moved. He was also very keen to film the children. "But they don't know what's happening to their father," I objected.

"That doesn't matter. We'll just show them sitting with you on the sofa — and ask after him."

"Fine," I agreed. So I sat with the children on the sofa in

our sitting room, flicked through picture books with them and let the journalist ask me, in front of the camera, when Raif was finally going to join us. Later the editor cut these shots together with the rest of the interview that I had already given him.

From the finished video file that the editor sent me, it seems quite clear that I was feeding the children all kinds of lies. So I was careful to ensure that they didn't get their hands on it. After I'd watched it for the second time I deleted it from the hard disk.

Abu Raif also learned from the media about the judgment against his son. And he too was unhappy about it: he thought it was too lenient. He loudly announced as much in various videos, filmed himself as always. And he wasn't letting up in his demand for guardianship of his grandchildren: he absolutely wanted to get his hands on Raif's and my children. Presumably he saw this as an opportunity to force Raif morally to his knees.

He contacted the authorities and officially announced his desire to fetch the children away and take control of their education. The problem was that under Saudi law he was in the right. So the authorities had to leap into action. And as it was general knowledge that I was living in Lebanon with the children, the Saudi embassy in Beirut was given the task of contacting me.

One day in late summer I got a call on my mobile. "Are you Ensaf Haidar, the wife of Raif Badawi?" asked a man's voice.

Suspicious as I was by now, I didn't reply, but waited until he went on talking.

"I work at the Embassy of the Kingdom of Saudi Arabia,"

he said. On a spontaneous impulse, I immediately hung up the phone. My whole body was quivering. So they had found me. Damn. I first had to sit down and light a cigarette. Damn. Damn. Damn. This was something different from anonymous threatening phone calls. Now the Saudi government was on our heels: the children and I were no longer safe here.

I frantically wondered what I could do. Getting a new phone number was the easiest exercise: you could buy them for ten dollars at the kiosk. But did they know where I lived? I found myself keeping watch on the street in front of our house. Was there a suspicious vehicle anywhere to be seen? The children were still at school. Should I make them come home at all? Would the member of the embassy staff come here and take them away? I was aware of my stomach tightening at the idea. But it was a distinct possibility.

At first I wanted to go straight to the school to pick them up and take them somewhere safe. But then I remembered that I had deliberately kept our new address a secret from the embassy. So that was why they had called me! They were looking for us. We had a small advantage — still. I had to use it. Above all I couldn't succumb to panic, I had to act in a considered fashion. As Raif would have done, I thought.

Oh, Raif! I had never missed him as much as I did right now. If I had at least been able to exchange a few words with him, I would have been calmer. But as it was I felt the huge burden of responsibility resting on my shoulders. I had to rescue my children from this monster who called himself their grandfather. And I was entirely on my own.

First I called the school and told them that a friend would be picking the children up that day. They must not go with any stranger apart from her, I told the headmaster. Then I dialed the number of the lawyer at the United Nations who had been so nice before. I told her I urgently needed to talk to her. "I'm busy right now," she started, but I wouldn't be fobbed off.

"It's very, very urgent," I insisted. "I'm already on my way to Beirut."

"All right then," she said, giving in.

She received me in her container office. This time I didn't have to draw a number. "What's so urgent?" she asked, when I was sitting opposite her at her desk.

I told her about the latest developments. About Raif's new sentence, about the threatening phone calls, about the demands that Raif's father was making, about the call from the Saudi embassy. I was very worried that the Saudi state would take my children from me, I admitted. That the long arm of the Saudi clerics could reach all the way here, to a foreign country. She understood the problem straightaway.

"Would you like me to arrange temporary alternative accommodation for you?" she asked me.

"That would be one possibility," I said. "But I'd rather leave the country with the children immediately."

She sounded thoughtful. "I can see that."

"Please help me!"

"I'll do what I can," she promised, and gave me an emergency number where I could contact her if anything unexpected came up. She also advised me to change my mobile number. "Don't answer any calls from strangers and don't go outside for the next little while," she insisted. "We'll act as quickly as possible."

"How quickly?" I asked her despondently.

"We have to wait until a country accepts you and the

children as refugees," she said—as she had at our very first meeting. I looked at her, discouraged. "But don't worry. I have a possible way of speeding up the process."

"Have you got children?" I asked her all of a sudden.

"Yes, one."

"Then you know what I'm talking about. But children don't deserve to lose both their father and their mother." I took her hand and looked her right in her pretty brown eyes. "Have mercy on those three innocent little creatures. Their fate lies in your hands."

# CHAPTER SEVEN

# ALMOST LEVEL WITH THE SUN

C anada. That was the name of the country that wanted to take us in. Canada had declared itself willing to grant us asylum. And I didn't think twice when the nice lawyer gave me the good news on the phone just two weeks after our conversation. "I'm so grateful to you," I said. "When can we go?"

I didn't know much more about Canada than its geographical location. Along with the children I looked for the place that we were supposed to travel to: Quebec. Dodi found a Wikipedia entry and told us that they spoke French there. I was glad of that; it meant that my children wouldn't have to start right from the beginning. He also told me, beaming, that there was a big chocolate factory there. He looked for photographs of the area on Google Images and showed them to his sisters. "It's very pretty. And there's a lot of snow in the winter," he explained to us. Miriam was particularly pleased about that. All three were infected with travel fever again.

I was surprised at how relaxed and optimistic the children were about the news of our new move. Inevitably they asked me why we weren't waiting for their father. Wasn't he coming along?

"Of course he's coming along," I reassured them. "It's just going to take him a while, unfortunately. He has a lot of work to do with his network. That's why we're meeting him there."

"Hm," Najwa, the eldest, said skeptically. "And when will that be?"

"How am I supposed to know? He's still busy getting rid of the flat. But he'll follow after us anyway. Wherever we go."

"Promise?"

"You can depend on it."

An information evening about Canada was being held in the UN refugee office. I went with the children. We learned lots about the country that was to be our new home: about the currency, the climate, the public transport system, people's habits. Even so, we still couldn't imagine what awaited us. Neither I nor the children had ever traveled to North America or to a European country. We had only ever seen the pale-skinned people who lived in those countries from a distance, when they had gone stomping through Cairo or Beirut as tourists. And now we were to live among them.

The UN refugee office also offered us the money for the tickets. Later we were to pay it back at a rate of a hundred euros per month. After I had put all our papers in order, at the end of October 2013 I booked a flight via Frankfurt to Montreal. Raif was infinitely relieved when the date was finally fixed. At last we would be able to escape the clutches of both our families for good.

"I can't tell you just how glad I'll be when I know you're safe at last," he said to me. "After that they can do what they like to me. I won't care." He had said it off the cuff. But his unconsidered remark told me that Raif didn't hold out very much hope for himself.

"Are you crazy? How can you say something like that?"

"I didn't mean it like that," he claimed. "I just want you to be OK."

"Has anything new happened?" I asked suspiciously. "Anything I should know about?"

"No." He fidgeted around. "Well, yes."

"What's up?"

"Maybe you could give Samar a call. Something seems to be up with Walid."

After we had hung up I rang Samar and Walid's number in Jeddah. Raif had told me that his lawyer hadn't called him for a long time. But he didn't know the reason why. It wasn't a good omen, so soon before our departure. Was Walid ill or something?

It was Samar on the line. "Oh, Ensaf," she said. She sounded glad to hear my voice, almost warm. At least not as brisk as I found her normally. Apparently she had been waiting for my call. "I'm sure you'd like to talk to Walid."

"Raif's worried because he hasn't heard from him for so long."

"Yes," said Samar — and then let the cat out of the bag: "He's been arrested himself."

"For heaven's sake!"

"They questioned him for two days, but then released him again."

"Well, thank God for that. Is he all right?"

"More or less," she said. "They weren't exactly gentle with him." She didn't go into details. But I could imagine it. I had been there often enough when Raif came back from those "interrogations."

"Is he at home now?"

"No, he's in Riyadh. His trial began a few days ago."

I was startled. "What trial? What are they accusing him of?"

"A load of nonsense. Dishonoring the authorities, unauthorized foundation of human rights associations—they mean the ACPRA—damaging the reputation of the state by communicating with international organizations and…"—she sobbed—"disobedience toward the king and attempting to undermine his legitimacy."

"Oh, no!" I exclaimed. When the Saudi Civil and Political Rights Association—ACPRA for short—was set up in 2009, Walid had been involved, but hadn't played a particularly significant role. The founding fathers of the organization, who attacked the practice of torture in the kingdom, for example, all came from the academic sphere, they had professorships and doctorates. This and the other charges were therefore less serious than the last one: disobedience toward the king was considered a capital crime. And, the thought suddenly occurred to me, a man who was accused of that particular crime couldn't seriously defend anyone else. All of a sudden Walid was completely discredited as a lawyer.

I didn't voice my thoughts, because I wanted to spare Samar's feelings. She was bound to be terribly worried about her husband. "What do the two of you want to do now?"

"Defend ourselves, what else?" she said laconically. "Walid is used to it." She tried to make it sound as if it wasn't such a big deal. As if such events happened in her life all the time — and she always survived them. I think that was how she saw it herself, so that she could bear it more easily.

But I was speechless. It was so easy to see her point of view. I knew exactly how it felt when your husband was up before the court. "I'm so sorry, Samar," I said. "Don't give up hope."

"Walid is very experienced," she repeated. "It isn't the first time they've tried to make things hard for him."

"Yes, of course."

"He'll fight his way out of this one soon too. And then he'll be able to turn his attention to Raif again."

"*Insha'allah*," I said.

One October morning we set off with all our belongings, four suitcases in all. A Lebanese friend brought me and the children to the airport. We spent hours going through the emigration formalities with a UN official. Then at last we were ready for check-in. We took our seats in a plane for Germany and crossed the Mediterranean. It was strange for me to leave the Arab world behind at that precise moment of uncertainty. But the children cheered as we broke through the clouds.

"Now we're almost level with the sun," Dodi explained to me.

I stroked his head and looked out the window with him. "It's a bit higher, in fact," I told him, "but we have got a little bit closer."

At Frankfurt airport another UN official welcomed us and helped us through passport control. It was already evening. Then we had almost nine hours to stroll around the shops and try out all the different perfumes in duty free.

Soon my children smelled as if they had all been bathed in a whole pond full of scent. But at least it kept them busy for a while. I was worried about losing them in the vast halls of the airport building. Particularly my little, curious Miriam, who at the age of six was especially adventurous and forever running away from me.

The later it got, the more crotchety the children became. For a while I managed to keep them in a good mood with crisps and Coca-Cola. But eventually they were full, and dozed exhaustedly on the benches.

At last things got going again very early in the morning. The next plane brought us from Frankfurt to Toronto. The flight was quite long, eight or nine hours in all. At first the children were delighted with all the films they were able to watch. But after a while they went to sleep in their seats. I didn't sleep a wink; I had too much on my mind. I looked at my three for a long time as they slept cuddled up together. What a life Raif and I had imposed on our little ones. And how imperturbably they went with us. My heart overflowed with love for our wonderful children.

We had another three long hours to kill in Toronto. But this time we just sat around wearily. When we landed in Montreal at last we were absolutely exhausted. By now we had lost all sense of time. Luckily there was a UN official in Montreal as well, who sorted out the immigration formalities for us. He had already booked a room for us in a hotel, and we went there by taxi. The kind Canadian even brought us packed lunches in case we felt hungry on the way. But when we reached the room we just threw ourselves down on the huge double bed and, exhausted, fell asleep.

We slept until the next morning, when we were woken by

the ringing of the telephone. I let Najwa answer, because she spoke French better than any of us. The lady at reception told her that the man from the United Nations was already there and waiting for us in the lobby. We had just enough time to get our things together and put on our thick down jackets, which I had bought in Lebanon. The packed lunches stayed untouched in the fridge. Our journey continued.

The UN official took us to Montreal bus station, which meant crossing the whole vast city. And unlike the previous day, my children were awake now and greedily absorbing the first impressions of their new home. They loved the water that surrounds the city on all sides, and the huge bridges that stretch across it. And they were very impressed with the urban canyons and skyscrapers downtown. In comparison with Lebanon many of the buildings in the center looked larger than life.

There was greater confusion about our future home. The children were a bit grumpy the first time I told them we were going to move to Quebec. I had meant the Canadian state. The children, however, had looked up the city of Quebec on the Internet. And now the UN official revealed to us that our final destination was to be a little town called Sherbrooke. It was in the state of Quebec, but it wasn't the city itself. "Why are we going there? We thought we were going to Quebec," they protested.

"But here in my papers it says you're going to Sherbrooke," the official objected.

They fired question after question at him to find out more about this mysterious place.

"What's it like there?" Najwa wanted to know. "Is it as pretty as Quebec?"

"Of course," the man reassured her. "You're going to love it."

"Is it like here in Montreal?"

"Not quite. It's a small town with quite a lot of students. There's a university there, and lots of cafés."

Najwa nodded and translated what he had said for my benefit. Meanwhile Dodi was busy calculating how far the little place was from the chocolate factory that they had been looking forward to so much. "If it isn't very far, maybe we could have an outing to it, what do you think, Mum?" he said instantly, busy trying to negotiate with me. He has an infallible sense for when the time is right.

I could hardly refuse his wish. "Of course we'll do that," I promised him.

At the bus station the man bought us tickets. The children kept asking questions about Sherbrooke: they asked the people who were waiting for the bus with us whether they lived there and what the place was like. They are, as I've said, very sociable. So soon the whole station knew what our plans were. Complete strangers gave us their opinion about Sherbrooke, and offered us tips about what you could do there. But luckily they all agreed that it was a lovely place.

The UN official wished us the best of luck in our new life. "Don't worry. With such intelligent children you'll find your feet very quickly," he said to me in English. But because I don't speak the language very well I was hardly in a position to reply to him. Still, I was able to tell him via Najwa how grateful we were to him for his help.

Then the bus set off. The children used the two-hour journey for an exhaustive photographic session. They were excited about the beautiful landscape with all the water, the brightly colored leaves on the trees and all the green, which they only knew from foreign films. Each of them borrowed my phone in turn and took pictures of the little houses past which we drove. They wanted to send the photographs to their father, so that he could get used to his new home in advance. "After all, he's got to know where he's going. Not that he knows as much as we do. We've got to tell him that we aren't going to be living next to the chocolate factory," said Dodi. But I was pretty sure that his father would be able to take this blow reasonably well.

When we drove into Sherbrooke, my three fell quite silent. They stared mesmerized out of the window. The town is set amid the hills along a big, wide river, which we crossed on a bridge. Our informants hadn't exaggerated: Sherbrooke is a really pretty town.

When we got out at the bus station we found ourselves walking into a very cold wind. The children pulled up the zips of their anoraks. We weren't used to weather like that.

A plump woman in a headscarf and a tall man with Arab features came toward us and introduced themselves as Fadila and Mohammed. Fadila works for Service des nouveaux Canadiens, an organization looking after all new arrivals to Canada. She originally comes from Algeria, and she had been living in Canada for seven years. Her husband Mohammed had been there longer.

"Welcome to Sherbrooke," said Fadila, and kissed me by way of greeting. She treated us as if we were best friends and had known each other for a long time. I found that incredibly reassuring. She and Mohammed immediately gave us the feeling that we weren't completely alone in this new world.

They drove me and the children to a little hotel near the

main street of Sherbrooke, where we were to spend the first few days. Called the Hotel Wellington, it was little more than an old shack, but it was clean. We were at least able to rest there a little — and we could finally tell Raif where we were. A day later he reached us via the central number of the hotel.

"It's all fine," I reassured him. "We've arrived safely."

"How are the children?"

"They think Sherbrooke's great."

"It's just a bit cold!" Najwa called out from behind me.

"And the chocolate factory is much farther away than we thought," Dodi added.

"I'm sure it's a beautiful place," he said.

"When are you coming, Dad?" Miriam wanted to know.

"As soon as you've explored everything, I'll be with you."

"That's what you said to me in Lebanon," Najwa remarked.

Raif ignored his oldest child's criticism. "Do as your mother tells you, you three," he told them. "Promise?"

"Yes, promise, Dad," said Dodi. "But come soon. We miss you. And Mum needs you, because it's very cold here. So cold that you can't even imagine it back home."

Dodi's description summed up the place very well: we were in good shape, but we were suffering terribly from the drop in temperature. In Canada it is already bitterly cold at the beginning of November. At that time of year the snow starts falling too — and it settles for several months. So we had the whole hard winter in front of us.

Fadila was an angel, helping me with just about everything in those early days. At first she supported me in finding a flat. I looked at two flats and then took the third one because it was the roomiest. It was in the basement, but it had two children's rooms and another bedroom. All five of us would be able to live there if Raif came.

I must admit that the flat didn't quite come up to my expectations. Presumably most people feel like that when they've just arrived from abroad: you've seen so many American films that you automatically assume that all the people on the continent live in spacious, elegantly furnished palaces — and you'd like one as well. I only realized that there were lots of poor people in North America when I myself became one of them. But I swallowed my disappointment at the selection. The most important thing was that the children and I had somewhere to stay, and could pay for it with the social aid that the state gave us.

Fadila and two other volunteers from her organization helped me to clean our little empire and furnish it with the basics. I don't know how, but they managed to get hold of a used stove, beds and mattresses, a kitchen table and a minimum of crockery, as well as towels and bed covers. At first we didn't have a washing machine or a television; I acquired those things later. I told the children that I deliberately didn't want to furnish everything perfectly, as their father might have his own ideas about how he wanted things to be when he turned up. They exchanged significant glances. Their skepticism was written on their faces. But I myself believed what I was saying to them: on all our many stops I had always had a feeling that we hadn't really arrived yet. I would only believe I was truly home when Raif was with us again.

Fadila also helped me with lots of other things that needed sorting out. As I spoke only Arabic, I was totally dependent on her help, particularly with all the paperwork. She helped me register with the city administration, to apply for welfare, to find affordable health insurance and register at the hospital. She and her husband also took me with them when they drove to the supermarket to do the weekly shop. Being able to put everything I needed for my children in the boot so I didn't have to carry it all the way home was a great relief to me.

For the children, Fadila recommended me a public school very nearby. We enrolled them there together. All three had to do an assessment test to decide what classes they would attend. But they were only able to start school after Christmas. So in the first month we spent a lot of time at home, while more and more snow fell outside. It really looked very beautiful. At least if you were looking at it from the kitchen window, and not standing right outside in the cold.

Oh, the cold. That first year the icy climate was particularly hard to bear. The children were braver than me: I dressed them in long trousers and gloves, and bought them caps that covered their faces down to their eyes. Out they went dressed up like that to build snowmen. Or else they went sleigh-riding with the neighbors' children. I found the change in climate harder to deal with, and avoided staying outside if I could. All those visits to the authorities were quite enough for me.

We spent Christmas with our friends from the Service des nouveaux Canadiens. Volunteers had organized a party for everyone who didn't have anywhere to celebrate otherwise. We listened to Christmas carols and stories about Father Christmas, which I didn't understand a word of. There were presents too: Najwa got colored pencils for her drawing, Dodi a toy car and Miriam the new Barbie doll that I had owed her for so long. We were all given a packet of sweets and other treats.

I thought the party was a very nice gesture for us new arrivals. The Canadians wanted to give us the feeling that we belonged there. And yet in the depth of my heart I realized that I felt very alone. I almost felt guilty. I didn't want to be ungrateful, but there was nothing I could do about it. I felt lonely, an outsider, among all these friendly people.

Raif was missing. There was no news from Jeddah, either good or bad. The appeal proceedings were suspended. Walid was now a free man again, but because the charges against him had been upheld, there wasn't much he could do as a lawyer. Was there any hope that my husband would be with us soon, as I constantly told everyone? Was I just putting on a show, especially for the children?

I realized in the course of the winter that I was slowly sinking into depression. It crept up on me as the initial stress with the authorities slowly ebbed away and I didn't have so much to do. I could hardly handle it. At the same time I knew I couldn't give up and just accept my fate. I owed that much to Raif and my children. So I pulled myself together.

Fadila suggested that I enroll in a French course to learn the language — and maybe meet a few people at the same time. I agreed. But before it began, I had one request: I knew that for some time an Amnesty International group in Norway had been taking an interest in Raif's case. "Would you help me contact the people from Amnesty here in Canada?" I asked Fadila. "I somehow have to support Raif. It makes me furious, sitting here all the time and doing nothing while he's in jail."

I didn't need to explain to her for very long. Fadila understood me straightaway. "Have you had contact with them already?"

"Yes, in Lebanon," I told her. Back then, after Raif's first accusation of apostasy, someone called May had rung me from London, after a few keen human rights activists had held a tiny demonstration in Oslo. She had interviewed me on Skype and put together a small file on Raif's case. I hadn't heard from her since then.

"Well, then we've got an excellent starting point," said Fadila.

One afternoon when the children were in school, we met at my house and found the number for Amnesty's London headquarters on the Internet. Since Fadila also spoke English, she rang on my behalf. She had herself put through directly to May. It was all surprisingly easy. May had to think for a moment about who I was, but then she remembered our conversation and Raif's case. She was very pleased that I had called, and gave Fadila the number of the Amnesty office in Sherbrooke which, she told us, had just been opened. We could contact one Mireille Elchacar. Fadila noted the number and thanked her very much.

"Look, they've even got an officer here in Sherbrooke," she said triumphantly after she had hung up.

"Right, let's give her a call before the children get back," I said impatiently.

"Hold your horses, Ensaf. I'm already on the case."

Mireille had time to meet me that afternoon. She's now one of my best friends in Sherbrooke — and we like to remember the first day we met. As she had just come off maternity leave and only recently started working for Amnesty in Sherbrooke, she still didn't have a proper office. So she invited me to her house. Fadila brought me and the children to the address she gave her.

Yes, me *and* the children. They had just got out of school and I didn't know where to put them. So I brought them along. Mireille later told me, laughing, that she hadn't been quite sure at first which of the visitors standing by her front door was the mother, and which were the children.

Of course she's exaggerating, even though I'm really not much bigger than my big children.

"*Alan, keif al hal?*" said Mireille — and at first I thought I had misheard. Had she just spoken Arabic?

"*Al-hamdullilah,*" I answered automatically. "I'm fine. Do you actually speak Arabic?" Mireille is a tall, slim woman with long black hair, pale skin, a narrow face, a big nose and light brown eyes. But her manner and her way of dressing looked entirely Canadian. "You aren't an Arab, are you?"

Mireille laughed and explained to me — in slightly halting but error-free Arabic — that her family came from Lebanon. She had emigrated with her parents and gone to school in Canada. That was why her Arabic sounded a little rusty at first — and Dodi loved pulling her up on it. But now she speaks as fluently as if she had just arrived from Beirut.

Fluent or not, I was very relieved to be able to speak to Mireille in my own language. "I'll leave you alone then," said Fadila, who had come along to translate, but actually had plenty of other things to do.

Mireille invited us into her sitting room and brought coffee. I tried to explain my case to her as the children went charging around us, but I couldn't really say what was what in front of them. So I resorted to hints. I also spoke very quietly, because I thought that way my children wouldn't hear me. But Mireille couldn't hear me either. She thought at first that perhaps her Arabic wasn't good enough to understand me. And we did speak different dialects. But eventually it dawned on her that it was because the children were there that I was speaking so quietly, and in riddles.

She asked her husband to take the gang of rascals to the playground: my three and their own little son. Only their baby was allowed to stay. "So, what's up?" she asked me when everyone was out of the house. I told her the whole story: about Raif's Internet platform, about his arrest, about the accusations of apostasy and the terrible sentence according to which he was due to be given six hundred lashes.

"For heaven's sake," she said emotionally, and held my hand tightly. "That's barbaric."

I almost wept with relief at finally being able to confide in someone. Someone who knew about these things and understood me.

Mireille was very interested in Raif's case, and started undertaking very detailed research. I would like to say it quite explicitly here: If Raif is ever freed without having been whipped to death, this woman will be largely responsible.

The next time Raif called me I told him about my initiative. He was excited. "You've done a great job, Ensaf!" he said. "It was really a great idea of yours. If Amnesty takes on the case, we may have a chance. The organization is very influential and with the help of public opinion it might be able to put pressure on the Saudi government."

I only understood half of what Raif was saying, but I was glad that my foray had apparently given him fresh hope. Perhaps that's normal, when you're in prison: eventually you think the whole world's forgotten all about you. Any sign that you still have a part to play in the outside world becomes terribly important.

"Just be happy that you've got me," I teased him, because even if you're talking on the phone to a prisoner, a joke of some kind has to be permitted. At any rate, in spite of all the horrors, Raif and I have never lost our sense of humor. "Or do you perhaps imagine that another woman would go to all this trouble?"

"No, Ensaf," he said, swearing his undying love over and over again. "You're unique."

Mireille had a copy of Raif's file sent from London. It was a tiny dossier, which tried to tell his story in barely half a page of text. She wouldn't settle for that: on several mornings when the children were in school she invited me to her house and asked me to talk to her in great detail about the course of events — from the small beginnings of Raif's activity as a journalist to the absurd turns that the case had assumed in the Saudi courts.

She also carefully recorded Walid's problems with the law. By now the court in Mecca had confirmed his sentence of three months' imprisonment for disregard of the legal authorities. But he was a free man again. Walid also faced trial in Riyadh, where far more serious charges had been made against him. This trial, in which his alleged disobedience against the king was the most serious charge being leveled, hung over his head like a sword of Damocles.

Mireille recorded everything. On the basis of my statements she produced a new, wide-ranging report, in which she judged both the trial against Raif and the one against Walid to be politically motivated. That was the first step. Then the organization decided to intensify its concern with the two men's problems.

One important strategy used by Amnesty is to personalize

the overriding political goals that the organization stands for. Of course Amnesty had been attacking the inhuman policies of the Saudi regime and its practice of torture for a long time, Mireille explained to me. But while there was no concrete, individual destiny to make this injustice clear, no one in North America was interested. In that sense Raif's fate provided a very welcome example that made the injustice highly visible. And of course the fact that I was there and was able to tell people about him helped as well.

In my sitting room we filmed a video with Luke, the cameraman, in which I delivered a brief address in Arabic: "I am Ensaf Haidar, the wife of Raif Badawi," I said. "My husband is in jail in Saudi Arabia for writing his opinion on the Internet. He has been unjustly sentenced. Fight with me for my husband." That was more or less the text that Mireille had drafted for me. Amnesty central office in London then made the video available to the organization's groups all over the world, so that they could use it for their publicity work.

That was how it started.

At the same time, through our work together Mireille dragged me out of my domestic isolation: as we are both around the same age and both have children there are many points of intersection. We often did things together that had nothing to do with our cause. She took me along when she went shopping for clothes for the children, and showed me the cheapest shops. Once we took the little ones off to see the maple harvest, which is a big spectacle in Canada. When the snow melts in the spring and the sweet sap rises in the trees, buckets are fastened to the tree trunks in the forests. The juice is then cooked over a fire to make a syrup that smells deliciously enticing, utterly irresistible to children. My three, at any rate, were very excited. Since then they have poured maple syrup over nearly everything they eat — but they love it best on cornflakes.

I made my first live public appearance with Amnesty International in mid-May 2014. Shortly before that, on May 7 to be precise, I had received very bad news from Saudi Arabia. Raif had called to tell me that the appeal proceedings had come to nothing. I got goosebumps whenever he expressed himself so cryptically, because it usually didn't bode well.

"What does that mean? What's the sentence?" I asked him anxiously.

"One thousand lashes, a fine of two hundred and seventy thousand dollars and ten years in jail," he replied.

That was a blow. I was speechless. After we had all agreed that action had to be taken against the previous sentence of six hundred lashes, since it seemed to us to be completely inhumane and unacceptable, the judges had cranked up the level of the sentence rather than allowing leniency to prevail. Our initiative had not only been in vain, it had had terrible negative consequences. Or rather: fatal consequences. Because no one could survive a thousand lashes. I couldn't believe that the judges had made such an unjust ruling.

I would have liked to hear Walid's opinion and ask him if he saw any possibilities for Raif. But he himself had been arrested during a trial and put in jail again without any further explanation. According to Samar he was in solitary confinement. Later we discovered that he had also been physically tortured through being deprived of sleep and constantly exposed to light.

In the face of all this injustice it is hard not to despair. I no longer had any idea how to give Raif courage. Given the relentless vengefulness of the Saudi legal system I felt small and helpless. What could I do to counteract this murderous regime?

Raif and I saw only one way out: publicity. "Go to this Amnesty event," Raif begged me before they took him from Briman prison, where he was in investigative custody, to permanent imprisonment in al-Ruez. "Tell the world what happened here. Tell everyone!"

"You can depend on it, *habibi*," I promised.

So I drove with Mireille to Montreal where Amnesty International's general assembly was to take place. They wanted to present Raif's case there — and introduce me to the whole team. For the benefit of my three children I had disguised the whole thing as an outing. They sat in the backseat while we drove to the provincial capital in Mireille's car.

To keep from revealing to them what we were actually planning to do in Montreal, Mireille and I had to be very careful about what we said. I fidgeted uneasily in my seat, felt terrible stage fright and was desperate to bombard Mireille with questions. Unusually, I couldn't wait for the moment when I could entrust my three to Amnesty's childcare.

Mireille had already told me off several times for not telling the children the truth. "They have a right to know who and where their father is," she said to me. "Why don't you come clean with them?"

"Because they wouldn't understand," I answered. "Because they would be shocked. Because they think only criminals go to jail. And because their father doesn't want me to." I thought of a thousand reasons why the children's illusions must not be destroyed.

"Raif has nothing to be ashamed of," Mireille repeated

over and over again. But she respected my decision, even if she was of a different opinion.

When the five of us stepped into the entrance hall of the university where the assembly was taking place, I wished I could cover my children's eyes and push them back out again. Even Mireille recognized straightaway that we had made a mistake in bringing them here. Raif's face smiled down on us from all directions.

"Why is Dad in the posters?" Dodi asked immediately.

I was too shocked to give him an answer. But Mireille was serene. "Because your dad is a hero and because we want to talk about his work and his thoughts," she answered for me.

"What's Dad doing that makes people admire him so much?" Dodi pressed.

"He runs an Internet network and advocates freedom of expression."

Dodi nodded as if he understood. "Is that why he has no time to come and see us?"

Now Mireille didn't know what to say. Dodi's face darkened. "I think he's just forgotten us because he's too busy."

"No, he hasn't!" I answered shrilly. "How can you say such a thing?"

We quickly dropped the children off with the childminder to avoid any further questions. But all the way throughout the event I kept thinking about what had happened. I was worried about Dodi's questions. The children, it seemed to me lately, didn't just have doubts about the version of the story that I was clinging to so frantically. They were also increasingly developing internal resentment against their father because he didn't keep his promises. A few times they had even refused to talk to him on the phone when he called us. That made me think. Perhaps my tactic wasn't so clever after all.

Even so, my first appearance with Mireille went very well. Mireille presented Raif's case and the general situation of human rights activists in Saudi Arabia in a short PowerPoint presentation. Then she invited people to ask me questions, which she translated into Arabic for me. I answered them — and managed to conceal my nerves behind a façade of calm. Apart from the Amnesty members, lots of students from the university also listened to the presentation.

At the end of the event the students gave me a present. They had painted Raif's face on a big canvas, with the words *"Libérons Raif"* — let's free Raif — underneath. They had also all signed their names. I was delighted and decided to hang the picture above the sofa in our sitting room. I told the children, truthfully, that Raif's admirers had made it for us. Dodi looked skeptical again.

"And why are they demanding freedom?" he probed.

"Well, because your father argues for freedom and human rights. You know that," I told him.

"Has he got problems at home?"

"Not big problems," I claimed, and repeated like a mantra what I always told him: "I'm sure he'll be with us soon."

All summer Mireille and I went tirelessly around providing information in the area around Sherbrooke. In her little car we zipped around from school to school, college to college, telling people about Raif's case and talking with the students about the situation in Saudi Arabia. Every week we were invited somewhere else.

Soon we were a practiced team. Mireille took over the presentation of Raif's case. "First his blog was tolerated by the government, and Raif even used his real name," she told the students. "But the situation in Saudi Arabia changed radically with the Arab Spring: in 2012 his blog was closed down, and now no one dares to publish critical texts under their real name." She went on to explain to the audience the demands Amnesty International was making in political terms. These are overriding goals such as freedom of the press, a prohibition on torture and the condemnation of the death penalty. As a precautionary measure to avoid inflaming the Saudi Arabian government against us any further, I couldn't explicitly support these political demands—I was only available for questions from the audience that specifically concerned Raif.

Mireille translated for me. But as I was now industriously attending French classes, I myself was getting much better at understanding what was going on around me.

I was moved by the students' questions. "Does Raif know about your campaign?" a young woman asked me.

"Yes," I told her. "When we speak on the telephone I tell him about it. And it gives him great hope to think that the world hasn't forgotten him. I am to pass on greetings from him to all of you, and thank you on his behalf for your support."

The students applauded my words. "What role does a lawyer have in the Saudi legal system?" asked a woman with long blonde hair.

This time Mireille answered for me. "That's what we're all wondering! Raif's lawyer wasn't even able to talk to Raif during the trial. And now he is in jail himself, because he allegedly undermined the legitimacy of the king. Isn't that right, Ensaf?"

"Yes, that's right." Shortly beforehand a heavily pregnant Samar had called me and told me tearfully that a special court had sentenced her Walid to fifteen years in prison, followed by a fifteen-year travel ban and a fine of fifty thousand dollars. "Disobedience to the ruler and attempted undermining of his legitimacy," it said right at the top of a long list of Walid's supposed crimes. He was also charged with insulting the legal system, founding prohibited associations, sullying the reputation of Saudi Arabia by communicating with international organizations and spreading information that endangered public order. Samar was in despair. To cap it all, she feared that her father might apply for guardianship over her again — and that he might even get it. Her only hopes now rested on her uncle, who had been granted guardianship over her before she married Walid. But if Walid didn't resist the intervention by Mohammed Badawi stubbornly enough, things looked very bleak for Samar.

"The last time sentence was passed, Raif stood completely alone in front of the judge," Mireille reported.

"Will this unjust system change if we manage to free Raif?" the student wanted to know. The question was clearly directed at me.

"I would suggest that we get him out first. Then let's see what happens next," I replied diplomatically.

"What are you asking of the Canadian government?" was the next question from a student sitting in the audience.

"I'd rather not answer that," I said, and pointed to Mireille.

"Ms. Haidar is a refugee in our country," she explained to the young people. "So she wants to refrain from making political demands on the government. But I can tell you

Amnesty's position on this topic. We demand that the Canadian government reappraise its relationship with Saudi Arabia, and put more pressure on the government in Riyadh."

I nodded, and the students applauded again. At the end of the event many people added their names to Amnesty's list of signatures, which Mireille had placed by the entrance to the auditorium.

Mireille's information campaign saved me first of all: it gave me the feeling of doing something meaningful for Raif, in spite of the apparently hopeless situation. And in fact our appearances were becoming more and more famous, first in Sherbrooke, then in the surrounding towns and villages and finally in Montreal as well. More and more people were interested in his case and demanding his liberation.

Whenever Mireille and I came to an information evening in some small town, the local press showed up too. Since not much happened in these little towns they were only too happy to write about Raif's case. I willingly gave interviews to the reporters. Constant dripping wears away the stone, I said to myself. And in fact I brought the story of Raif's fate to the attention of more and more people all over Canada.

We also tried to make contact with local politicians. One of the first to receive me in his office and listen to the story was Pierre-Luc Dusseault, who represented Sherbrooke in the regional parliament. Fadila had agreed a date with him. "I'm very impressed with the way you're fighting for your husband," he told me. "If Raif is released one day, I'm sure he'll owe it to you," he said to my great delight.

On Mireille's advice I also started tweeting, and opened a professional Facebook account in which I kept the public systematically involved about the development of Raif's case.

A political friend of Raif's translated my texts into English so that they reached an international audience.

But it also enabled my family, from whom I had for good reasons kept my flight to Canada a secret, to find me again. My brothers and sisters and cousins were the first to subscribe to my communications. As soon as they had done so, they started causing problems once more. My brother Mohammed started threatening me again, as I had supposedly sullied his honor. And my sister Hanan's thirteen-year-old son wrote to me: "If I see you, I'll smash your face in."

"I'll do the same to you," I replied to the snotty little brat by return of post.

By now their threats worried me less because in Canada I felt reasonably safe from their attacks. In fact their statements struck me as ridiculous. They were behaving as if I'd made sex films and put them online. But luckily you can block your "friends" on Facebook: only people who didn't insult me had access to the forum.

My cousin Adel was among them. One day, when I was taking my second course of French lessons, I checked my phone during a break and read a post from him. "My beloved uncle died today," he wrote. The message made me freeze. Adel's beloved uncle was none other than my father.

My father had died, and I had to read it by chance on Facebook. A wave of sadness washed over me. I asked the teacher for permission to stay away from the rest of the lesson that day and went home. I lay around helplessly in the flat and didn't know what to do with myself or my feelings. Because regardless of whether or not there was a family argument, my father was still my father. And the news of his death hurt me. Very much, in fact. But I couldn't weep.

I looked at my Facebook account. Would anyone from my family send me condolences? So far I hadn't received any message along those lines. I doubted that my family had my phone number, but I was sure that they would send me a message of some kind. I waited calmly for something to arrive.

But nothing came. In my helplessness I "liked" Adel's message. It was as if I was calling out to them. Hello! I have something to do with this too, I still exist! I waited all day and the next for a reaction. But no one moved. No one saw the need to inform me of my father's death, let alone pass on their sympathy. None of my sisters. Not my mother. No one.

I was an outcast. And you don't communicate with an outcast—not even to tell them that their father has died. However, two days later Adel managed a brief "My condolences, Ensaf." That was all that came. None of the rest of them has ever contacted me. I probably don't need to mention that I didn't receive any of my inheritance.

Their behavior hurt me terribly. What a family, how intransigent they are. What crime had I committed in their eyes?

# CHAPTER EIGHT

# THE HOUR OF TRUTH

"What are lashes, Mum?" Dodi asked me innocently one day. He used the Arabic expression *gelt*. It gave me a terrible start when he ambushed me like that.

"Where did you pick that word up?" I asked him, as I busied myself in the kitchen with a baking dish. I was just making dinner. But I had missed the right moment to take my work out of the oven. The cheese already smelled burned.

"From the Internet," said Dodi. "So what does the word mean?"

"Don't bother me with questions like that," I stalled. "Can't you see that I'm busy?"

"You don't want to tell me!"

"If you're spending all your time on the Internet, I'll take your tablet away," I threatened. "Go and get your sisters and tell them to help you lay the table. Am I the maid or something?"

That worked, and Dodi sloped away. A short time later he came back in with Najwa in his wake and began politely setting the table for dinner. But I knew very well that he and she had nothing more important to do in their room than scour the Internet for information about our family secret. They were on Raif's trail, and mine.

My own media campaign would give me away sooner or later: the more successfully I informed people in Canada about Raif's fate, the harder it was becoming to hide the whole thing from the children. They sensed very clearly that something wasn't quite right about their permanently absent father — and that applied equally to the voluble explanations I gave for his absence.

A long time ago they had started firing unpleasant questions at me. Dodi, particularly, kept putting me to the test. "If Dad is allowed to move to Canada, why doesn't he at least come and visit us?" he asked only a few months after our move to Sherbrooke.

From the way he said it I could tell that he must have found his grandfather's videos on the Internet. "There are a lot of nutcases on the Net," I told him. "Don't believe everything you see there!"

All three children had also seen the CNN interview I gave when we were still living in Lebanon. In it I had expressed my worst fears, and pleaded with the Saudi king to show mercy to Raif. At the time it hadn't occurred to me that they might be able to find my appeal two years later on YouTube. I cursed the editor who had insisted on filming the children as well. As a result they knew what to look for.

During the time that we had been parted from Raif, there had been many such moments of suspicion about my version of the story. And eventually, when suspicion got the upper hand, the children became really cantankerous: they were unbearable at home.

Dodi was particularly aggressive. He argued constantly with his sisters. His teacher even told me that he had recently started having problems with his fellow pupils. I was at my wits' end, so I asked a social worker what to do.

"Tell them the truth," she advised me — just as Mireille had done before. But I couldn't: Raif had explicitly asked me not to tell the children. It was incredibly important for him. Now that he was in jail and having to endure that terrible punishment, how could I not fulfil his deepest wish?

So I continued playing my game of hide-and-seek with them. But at the same time I tried to keep the campaign running and make an increasingly wide public aware of Raif's story. It was a curious balancing act. It almost consumed me from within. I brooded for nights on end about how I could protect the children against all the media reports I was provoking with my activities. My nightmare was that they would spot their father on the front page of some newspaper or other.

In the autumn, when the sentence of a thousand lashes for Raif was confirmed by another court, a friend of mine had an idea. Jane Hospes is one of the teachers at the institute where I take French lessons, and she had heard about my story when the teachers' union asked me for a talk. She was so impressed with my account that she gave me her private number afterward and offered to support me in any way she could if I needed help. Jane had heard that demonstrations for Raif's release had recently taken place in Scandinavia. "If they can get something going, then so can we," she said. "Don't you think, Ensaf?"

"Really?" I had doubts about whether there were really enough people in Sherbrooke who would take to the street for Raif. It had got painfully cold again in the meantime.

"Of course. I'll organize that for you," she offered. "You don't need to worry about it. But you've got to come."

I gratefully accepted the offer. Jane, who is almost twenty years older than me but a real bundle of energy, took care of all the things you need for a demonstration: posters, a megaphone, and a drum that makes a really loud noise, as well as thick gloves and caps. And of course the authorities had to be informed. What Jane had in mind was more a vigil than a demonstration: it was to take place in front of the mayor's office every week at Friday, at exactly twelve o'clock, the time when Raif would be flogged — if the people in Jeddah really did decide to flog him.

We started in December. In the middle of that winter's iciest weather a handful of us went and stood in front of the town hall. Jane had, as I said, had big posters printed. On each of them was a huge letter, eighteen in all. Each participant was to hold a letter aloft. With the letters we formed the demand *Libérez Raif Badawi!* — Free Raif Badawi! — and had our photographs taken by the local press.

Jane held up her megaphone and shouted: "Libérez Raif Badawi!" The demonstrators repeated her slogan. One of the activists drummed. Then Jane yelled, just in case the Arabic press was there too: *"Al hurria li Raif!"* The same demand in Arabic. The demonstrators repeated that too. It was an impressive performance. For the local press, who didn't often have anything exciting to report, it was probably the best story in years. Mireille also produced her own press release, of course.

Then she took me aside: "Many congratulations, Ensaf. Tomorrow you'll be the lead story," she said. My heart stopped for a minute. I absolutely had to hide the paper from my children, I thought. But it was also clear to me that the action in Sherbrooke would soon be the talk of the town. After all, from now on we planned to demonstrate every Friday.

So my social worker begged me to tell the children at last. When I still wouldn't take her advice, next time she visited she brought a psychologist with her.

"What's the best thing for the children?" I asked the man. He was an expert, so I was open to his advice.

"Your children need honest answers to their questions," he said. "If you go on lying to them, the situation at home and their relationship with you will only get worse. Tell them their father is a brave man." He thought for a moment. "A man like Nelson Mandela. Perhaps you could watch the film about Mandela with them. And then tell them that their father is in a similar situation as Mandela was then."

That sounded good. I promised him that I would mull over the matter. I would have liked to discuss the issue with Raif. But I couldn't, since he was strictly against it. So I talked about it to Fadila, who also advised me to take that step. Together we kept an eye out for the Mandela film. But as we couldn't find it anywhere in Sherbrooke, I finally summoned up the courage even without it.

I called all three children into the sitting room and told them I wanted to talk to them. "I need to tell you something important," I began. "But you must promise me that you will be strong."

They immediately noticed that I was serious, and nodded.

"I told you that your dad finds it hard to travel because of his network."

"Yes, because he has so much work to do," said Miriam politely.

"Exactly. Your father is a very strong man. He has used his network to fight for people in Saudi Arabia to be able to express their opinions freely." I cleared my throat. "And we came to Canada because we wanted to be free as well. Away from the constricting thoughts that prevail in our country." I broke off. What was I actually telling them? I tried to put my thoughts more simply so that they could understand them. "Well, so your father has always fought for freedom. And the government didn't like that. So they put him in jail."

They looked at me with big, shocked eyes. At that moment I felt terribly guilty about putting them through this. I didn't know what tormented me more, having lied to them for years, or now confronting them with the terrible truth.

They all reacted in completely different ways. Dodi was the first to find his voice again. "You see, I always knew," he said. "I saw Abu Raif's videos on YouTube. But you told us what he said wasn't true. You lied to me!" He was furious.

"But Dodi, what he says isn't true either," I defended myself. "Abu Raif says bad things about your father. But he hasn't done anything wrong. He only wrote his opinion on the Internet."

"You still lied," he insisted. "I've often told you that!"

Najwa didn't say anything. She just turned quite pale. And I could see from her face that she was terribly shocked and disappointed. She didn't ask me any questions. That was almost harder to bear than Dodi's attack of rage.

Little Miriam's reaction was perhaps the most natural: she started sobbing. I gave her a hug and told her she had to be a brave girl to help her father. She had a thousand questions. "What's it like in the jail where Dad is now?" she wanted to know. "What are they doing to him? Are they hurting him?"

"No, they're not hurting him," I lied and took my glasses, wet with tears, off my nose. "He's just sitting there and waiting until he can go again."

"But then we've got to help him. We have to go there and get him out!" she suggested.

Dodi shook his head. "They've got warders, dummy," he said, amused at his little sister's ignorance. "Do you think he'd stay there of his own accord if they didn't? We'd have to outwit them, at least." The two of them wondered how they could organize it.

"You know, I'm trying to help your dad all the time too," I said, and told them about the information events and my efforts to mobilize publicity. They thought that was good.

"Next time we'll come and demonstrate as well," said Dodi. "We want to be there too."

Najwa fell ill that evening. She complained of stomach pains, and had to spend a few days in bed. Even today she won't talk about the subject. Her two younger siblings, on the other hand, swung into action. Dodi asked me to tell him the exact details of the building in which his father was being held. He and Miriam developed a plan to free their father, in which her task was to distract the guards while he forced his way into his father's cell.

The two of them also shot propaganda videos on the tablet — very much in their grandfather's style: they put the camera on their table in the playroom and sat on two chairs in front of it. They pretended it was their "office," and started to deliver an address to the camera. "Ladies and gentlemen," said Dodi. "Our father hasn't done anything bad. He is a very brave man. He has devoted himself to making people free. That's why he's in jail. Please help us to get him out."

"Dear King," Miriam went on, "have mercy on our father and pardon him. That would really be a good deed for you to do." They were almost the same words she had heard me say in the CNN interview.

"And if you don't, I'll be very angry with you," Dodi added. "You just have to do it, because we miss him very much."

I clapped when they showed me the video. "Yes, fight for your father," I encouraged them. Because that was exactly what I wanted my children to be like: combative and brave. I tried not to show them any weakness, so that it wouldn't occur to them that sadness was an option.

It was only when they prepared to upload the video to the Internet that I had to stop them. Dodi's remarks about the king were too dangerous. "We'll ask Luke the cameraman to make a professional video with you — and then we'll use that in the campaign," I suggested. "What do you think of that?"

They were very excited. "Yes, I'm ready. Tell him to come soon so that we can get to work," Dodi urged me.

A great burden fell from my shoulders when I saw them reacting so positively: at last I could stop lying to them. In fact I could even involve them in the campaign. It was an incredible relief.

Now I just had to tell Raif, as gently as possible. I waited rather nervously until he was allowed to call us again. Luckily the children were at school. Then I admitted it to him: "I couldn't keep it secret any longer. They would have found out anyway," I said.

Raif was very annoyed, as I had expected. "That wasn't right. Why did you do it?" he asked me in exasperation.

"They would have found out eventually."

"You should have asked me first."

"We talked about it so often."

"Exactly. You knew I didn't want you to do it, and you did it anyway. What are they going to think of me now?" I think he felt very helpless because he couldn't control the situation himself. What his children thought of him was so important to him — and now that they knew he was in jail he thought they would have a bad opinion of him. "They'll think their father is a criminal. Do you think that'll do them any good?"

"They think the opposite, Raif. They think their father is a hero."

He couldn't hear me.

"And there was no option. Were they supposed to find out from the newspaper or something?"

He grumbled. And I understood that I would have to reassure him in some other way.

"Your children are on your side," I said. "They're proud of you and they're standing by you. Dodi and Miriam have even sat down and made a propaganda video calling for your release."

"Really?"

"Really."

"Did you tell them to do that?"

"I didn't say a word. It was their initiative. They really want to help you!" I told him that Dodi had arranged a shoot with Luke the following day. "He's spent all day writing a letter to you, and he wants to read it out."

"Hm."

"Would you like to hear it?"

Raif couldn't say no to that. I went to the table and fetched the sheet of paper that Dodi had covered with little penciled letters — and had already reworked several times.

"*Dad, I would never have thought I would have to be without you,*" I began reading to Raif. "*I would never have thought that you wouldn't be able to wake me up in the morning as usual to go to school. You're so far away from me, locked up in jail, because you have fought for all people to be able to say what they think. That's as far as he's got.*"

"Dodi wrote that?" Raif asked. He was clearly touched.

"As true as I'm sitting here and reading it out to you."

Raif didn't believe it until he'd asked the children themselves about it. "Did Mum tell you to make videos for me?" he asked Dodi, the next time they talked to each other on the phone.

"No. Miriam and I did that all on our own," said Dodi. "And we've come up with a plan to get you out — don't worry, Dad."

In the end Raif was reassured.

After these important things were finally out in the open, the situation at home relaxed. My children started behaving more affably, and we had a pleasant Christmas, our second in Canada. I baked cinnamon biscuits with them and made paper stars to decorate the house with, the tradition in our new home.


The New Year began with an act of violence. In Paris on January 7, 2015, two masked men stormed the editorial offices of the satirical magazine *Charlie Hebdo* and shot eleven journalists. The reason: in their caricatures they had supposedly insulted the Prophet Mohammed. That was what the

Islamists who carried out the bloody attack claimed. I was very familiar with that accusation from Saudi Arabia. Raif too had been accused of defaming religion in his blogs. But now the people who represented this radical set of ideas were rampaging even in Europe. The madness was spreading.

So I was very relieved to hear the next day that so many people had spontaneously taken to the streets in the evening to demonstrate against the massacre. Yes, I thought: quite right. Europeans must defend the freedom of the press. Otherwise journalists there will soon find themselves leading as fearful a life as journalists in my homeland.

A little later I called Raif. I will never forget that call as long as I live. It was on Thursday, January 8. "Have you heard about the attack in Paris?" I asked him.

"No." Raif clearly had something else on his mind. "Ensaf, I need to tell you something. Will you promise me that you'll be brave — and not tell the children?"

"Yes, of course." I sat down on a kitchen chair. I nervously fumbled a cigarette from the pack in front of me. What in heaven's name was coming now?

"Promise?" he asked.

"Yes. I promise."

"Tomorrow they're going to start enforcing my sentence. One of the warders told me."

It took me a moment to understand what he was telling me. "You mean...?"

"Yes, Ensaf. The first fifty lashes. I'll get them in front of the big mosque in Jeddah."

I didn't know what to say. Over the past few weeks I had completely repressed the idea that Raif was actually going to be whipped in addition to his prison sentence. I simply couldn't imagine the authorities going ahead with it. "That's impossible," I struggled to say.

"I'm afraid so, Ensaf," said Raif. "Promise me you'll stay strong?"

"Hm." What was I supposed to say? What do you say when the person you love tells you that he's going to be abused in the most horrible way?

"Don't worry. I'm tough," he said, apparently quite cheerful. "I can take pretty much anything. I'll call you as soon as I can. OK?"

"OK," I replied.

I can't describe how I felt after that conversation. I immediately called Mireille to tell her what I had found out. She was horrified too. "I'm so sorry, Ensaf," she said. "I wouldn't have believed that those bastards were serious."

I was crying all the time, unable to speak.

"Calm yourself, Ensaf," Mireille said helplessly. She couldn't bear it. "I know it's small consolation, but I promise you that the world will learn of this injustice," she said, and told me to post the news immediately on my Facebook account and on Twitter. She herself would use the channels of Amnesty International. "We have to shake people up," she said. "We can't have ten thousand people in Europe demonstrating for freedom of the press while at the same time a blogger in Saudi Arabia is being beaten to death."

Mireille sent our mutual friend Sylvie over so that I wouldn't be alone. She's older than me, and a kind of substitute grandmother for the children. So they were very happy when she came to visit us and even stayed overnight.

But I didn't sleep that night. I calculated the time difference between Canada and Saudi Arabia—and tried to determine the moment when that terrible day for Raif would begin. When would the prison warders wake him? When would they lead him in front of the mosque in handcuffs? Had they already started?

In the morning, before the children woke up, I confiscated all the computers, tablets and telephones in the apartment, and unplugged the television. I told the children that we were going to have a few media-free days, because they were watching too much television and spending too much time on the Internet. They sulked a little but accepted it. But when I told them they weren't to go to school that day, but spend the day with Sylvie, Jane and Jane's dogs, they were very excited. "Oh, great!" said Dodi, who is very fond of the creatures.

"Are you sure you don't want to come too?" Sylvie asked me, concerned.

I nodded. "I really can't, Sylvie."

"I can imagine that."

As soon as she had set off with them, I checked my Facebook page. It was full of declarations of solidarity with Raif and me: our friends were shocked at what was due to happen today. Lots of people had shared my message and passed it on. "It's a scandal," they wrote. Or "Stop this inhuman regime." Many also drew parallels with the attack on the *Charlie Hebdo* offices: "Both are acts of violence aimed at gagging journalists." And there were many other comments of that kind.

Then I turned on the television and waited for the lunchtime news. Mireille had done a great job: my husband was the second item, immediately after the events in France. I was disconcerted to see his familiar picture behind the face of a blonde newsreader. I can't even remember exactly what she said. But from her words I could tell that she didn't have much detailed information from Riyadh. It felt terrible, hearing her talk about Raif as if he was a random foreign news event. The whole day was one big nightmare.

I called Mireille. "Have they done it?" I asked her.

"Yes," said Mireille. "In public, in front of a big crowd of people. So we have witnesses. Soon it will be all over the Net."

"I just want to know how he is," I wept. But of course Mireille couldn't tell me.

"There's also supposed to be a video," she warned me. "Someone filmed Raif's lashes on their phone."

"Have you seen it?"

"Yes," she admitted. For Mireille the video that one of the onlookers had shot in the square in front of the mosque was a valuable document. But she advised me — as a friend — not to watch it. And I found the idea repellent anyway. No, I wouldn't inflict that on myself.

But after our conversation I found myself involuntarily searching the web. It wasn't hard to find. By now some of my Facebook friends were referring to it. It also appeared immediately on YouTube when you searched for "Raif Badawi" and "lashes."

It was as if I was being operated by remote control. With trembling hands I clicked on the video to set it in motion. I saw Raif's delicate frame from behind, in the middle of a big crowd of people. He was wearing a white shirt and dark trousers, and his hair hung down to his shoulders. He looked thin. His hands were cuffed in front of his body. I couldn't see his face. The men around him were wearing the usual white gowns, and shouting *"Allahu Akbar."* The innermost circle around him was formed of khaki-clad security men wearing police caps and carrying truncheons. One of them held him firmly in place.

Then the picture wobbled. Perhaps the person making the video had been jostled by a passer-by. Perhaps he had had to hide his phone from the police in the square for a moment, because of course what he was doing was illegal.

The next shot showed the punishment: again we saw Raif's back, quivering under the impact of the blows delivered by one of the security men. The man himself could not be made out in the video. But I saw clearly that he was striking Raif with all his might. Raif's head was bowed. In very quick succession he took the blows all over the back of his body: he was lashed from shoulders to calves, while the men around him clapped and uttered pious phrases.

It was too much for me. It's indescribable, watching something like that being done to the person you love. I felt the pain they were inflicting on Raif as if it was my own. The men I had seen in the video might as well have put me in a square and flogged me. But worst of all was the feeling of helplessness. I sat on my sofa, wrapped my arms around my legs and wept.

I don't know how long I sat there for. The phone rang several times, but I didn't answer. How was Raif now, I wondered. How severe were the wounds that he had suffered from this brutal abuse? Had they broken his bones? The violence of the blows almost made me suspect as much. Did he get medical treatment for his wounds? If only I could have done something for him!

Eventually the doorbell rang. Fadila was standing at the door. She looked into my tear-stained face and I didn't need to explain anything to her. She took me in her arms without a word. "Why are you sitting around on your own?" she scolded. "Sylvie and the others are getting worried because you don't answer the phone."

I sniffed.

"Come on, I'll make us some tea," she said and went into my kitchen to put the kettle on. She made tea with lots of sugar and cinnamon. Luckily the children were still out. Jane had taken them to a pizza restaurant.

"If I only knew how he was," I said to Fadila.

"I'm sure he'll call as soon as he can," she said, trying to reassure me.

In the course of the day and the evening more and more friends came to see me. All the people who had supported me in Sherbrooke wanted to be with me and show me that I wasn't alone. And yet I felt lonely in their midst. No one could comfort me.

Sylvie stayed with me for the second night, and was with me all weekend. I was very glad to have her there. Not least because of the children. They sensed quite clearly that I was feeling bad. "What's wrong, why are you so sad?" they asked me several times.

"She's just tired," Sylvie explained. "She's got a cold."

On Sunday morning we called Mireille, the only one of my close friends who couldn't come to see me because she had been working nonstop for Amnesty and our campaign since the announcement of the flogging. To be able to talk to her undisturbed, I took my phone out to our snow-covered terrace. With my free hand I tried to light a cigarette. I almost froze my fingers off.

"Ensaf, there's huge global interest in the story," Mireille told me. I already knew that from my own research on the Internet: all the big newspapers, television channels and news outlets had picked up Raif's story. On Facebook people were talking like mad about the injustice that had been done to him and to other journalists in Saudi Arabia. And against the background of the *Charlie Hebdo* attack and the huge mass demonstration that was being held in Paris that weekend, the subject developed a dynamic of its own: that representatives of the Saudi royal family were demonstrating side by side with François Hollande and Angela Merkel, while at the same time having a blogger whipped in their own country, was making people angry. "I'm getting a lot of questions from the editors. They all want to talk to you. Do you think you can do that?"

Given my condition I wasn't entirely sure. Appearing with Mireille in schools and universities and talking about Raif's situation had been one thing. But speaking out in public about his flogging was quite another. I was concerned that I was no longer emotionally capable of answering the questions that I was now being asked.

"Have a think," she said. "It would be very good for the campaign. That way we'll make Raif even more famous — and we might even be able to prevent them from going on whipping him next Friday."

Mireille didn't need to say anything more. "Of course," I replied. "At any rate, we've got to ensure that it doesn't happen again!" However I did ask her not to send the journalists until the children were back at school on Monday. "It's not meant for their ears."

"Ensaf, I don't know if we can go on hiding it from them. As I've told you, it's absolutely everywhere in the media. Perhaps you should gently make them familiar with it."

"Gently?" I asked shrilly. How, forgive me, do you tell your children "gently" that their father has been beaten in the cruelest way in a public square? I couldn't even tell them how Raif was, because I hadn't heard from him since then.

"Our decision on the subject — mine and Raif's — is quite firm," I told her.

"Just think about it," said Mireille.

In fact I managed to keep the children away from the Internet, from television and from the newspaper kiosks in Sherbrooke all weekend. On Sunday evening, however, the subject was still in the headlines, and I wondered whether I would even be able to send the children to school the next day. I woke them up at half past seven on the dot, as always. But as we were sitting together in the kitchen over cornflakes and maple syrup my phone rang.

"Ms. Haidar," asked a woman's voice. "Can you talk?" It was the principal of the school.

"Yes, of course." I dashed outside with the phone.

"I'm very sorry about what has happened to your husband," she began. "It's really terrible."

"Thank you for saying that."

"Dodi's class teacher is on the way to your house."

I was completely taken aback. "She's coming to see us?"

"Yes. All the children and teachers already know about what's happened. That's why I would ask you to come to school and see me on your own this morning so that we can discuss where we go from here."

"Fine," I said numbly. "See you soon."

A short time later there was a ring at the door and Dodi's class teacher, a nice young woman called Katja, came to visit us. Dodi, who was very fond of his teacher, was very pleased about this surprise. "Your mother still has some things to discuss with the principal. So I'll stay with you," she explained to the children. "What shall we do?"

Meanwhile I hurried to school. Even in the playground I noticed the other children looking at me and whispering. They knew very well who I was. They had all heard about the weekend's terrible events and seen the television reports. If this gang bothered me so much, how were my children going to fare? I didn't dare risk finding out. I wouldn't be able to send them to school for weeks. But what explanation could I give?

The principal had already assembled a council of teachers, a social worker and the school psychologist. "Thanks for coming," she said to me. "It's important that we think together about how to ensure that your children don't suffer any harm from this. You've already seen what's going on in the playground." I nodded. "That's why I would suggest that you leave your children at home today."

"Yes, that's better," I said, relieved.

"I suggest we organize things as follows," the principal went on. "The teachers and I, along with the psychologist, will talk to the pupils. We will ask them not to talk to your children explicitly about the subject when they come back. We'll say: We'd like you to meet them quite normally. Don't be either particularly curious or overly kind or even sympathetic."

"That's a good idea."

"And you must also use today to talk to your children." She scrutinized me for a moment.

"Meaning?"

"You've got to tell them what's happened."

"But I can't do that!"

"They'll find out anyway," she argued. "Children talk to each other. You can't stop them doing that."

"It's better if they find out from you," Robert the social worker tried to convince me. He offered to come home with me and jump in when I couldn't cope any more. "I'll help you find the right words."

I nodded mutely. I could see that there was simply no other way.

As we stomped back through the snow to my house, I kept thinking about Raif. My poor Raif, who lay somewhere in Jeddah, seriously abused, waiting for his wounds to heal. I still hadn't been able to talk to him; I assumed that his injuries were too severe for him to be able to call me. And while he was enduring all that, I had to inflict yet another wound: I had to break the promise I had given him yet again. I felt terrible. Like a traitor. But I had no choice.

Once I got home, I called the children together in the sitting room again. They already guessed that my serious face didn't bode well. "I need to tell you something," I said, and tried to find the right words. "Something bad happened this weekend."

"Is it about Dad again?" Dodi asked suspiciously. "Is that why we aren't allowed on the Internet?"

"How is he?" Najwa—already surprised that her father hadn't phoned at the weekend as he usually did—asked anxiously.

"He's fine," I lied. "Everything's great, but... The prison warders are very bad people. They, they..." I couldn't go on because with every word I wanted to say I immediately felt the tears welling up. And I didn't want to burst out crying in front of them. Robert leapt in and picked up the thread of the conversation for me.

"They've beaten your father," he told the children. They stared at him. "They have hurt him very badly. But now he's better again."

My children reacted very strangely to this new revelation. They didn't react at all. They stayed quite still and didn't ask any questions. Robert and Katja did their best to explain what had happened. But the children behaved as if they hadn't heard their words at all.

"We need to give them time to process all this," said Robert. The children took that time: they fell ill. All three complained of stomach pains and nausea. They didn't go to school for several days. But they remained persistently silent, even among themselves. Even today, no one in our house has ever talked about the subject again.

For almost a week we heard nothing more about Raif. During that week I gave interviews almost without interruption. The first were Skype interviews with Norway and Sweden, then German, French and South African journalists declared their interest. And of course all the Canadian radio and television channels. Mireille tried to coordinate the dates for me. I lost count of all the people she was guiding through our house. But there were journalists there all the time. Al-Jazeera sent a camera crew from Toronto. The BBC, the Lebanese broadcaster LBC and Deutsche Welle were also ready for action.

I willingly gave everyone information, and also let them film my flat—and the children. I considered it my duty to tell them everything they wanted to know. Because that was my most important goal: to create as much publicity as possible—and in this way perhaps to stop my husband being whipped to death over the coming weeks. Even today I am grateful to all those who came, because they took an interest in our fate.

Then all of a sudden, after almost a week, we received the call we were so desperate for. If I'm not mistaken it was a Thursday again when Raif was allowed to call us. His voice was weak, but he was trying to make it sound firm. "All OK where you are? How are you and the children?" he asked. I immediately started to cry.

"But Ensaf," he said soothingly. "You're not going to weep in front of the children?"

"How are you?" I sniffed. "Are you in great pain?"

"It's all fine. The wounds heal slowly."

"Are you receiving medical treatment?"

"Yes, a doctor examined me. He gave me a note saying that I'm not yet fit enough to be whipped again."

"Thank God," I said. Even if it didn't tell me anything good about Raif's physical state, at the same time it was positive news: at least this week they wouldn't be torturing him anymore. He couldn't tell me how things would go after that.

"Raif," I said, "the whole world is talking about your fate." I took a deep breath. "The children know about it too." Again the tears came. "There was nothing I could do about it. Believe me, I would rather have spared them all that too."

This time Raif's reaction was very understanding. He didn't level any accusations at me. "You're doing what you can. It's all my fault," he said. "How are they?"

"They're strong," I lied, "and full of fight."

"That's good," he said.

"Did you expect anything else? They're your children after all."

"You're right," he said.

My children and I are grateful for every day when they don't whip Raif again. After the first fifty lashes—and the international public outcry that followed—the men with the whips in Riyadh did not at first dare to repeat the punishment.

Since then our little flat in Sherbrooke has turned into a campaign office for Raif's liberation. It's here that we receive journalists and stay in contact with activists all over the world who are standing by us. Raif's face smiles from the banner over our sofa, while we get together to make posters for the next demonstration.

The children eagerly join in. They have become a constant part of my campaign. Of course at first I asked the journalists to take their feelings into account: Najwa, Miriam and Dodi don't like being asked to look sadly at the camera. What they have to bear is sad enough already. But they're always happy to deliver an intense—and noisy—plea for their father's release. My children don't like being put in the role of victim, and prefer to be feisty. Their father and I like them much better that way.

The international support that we have received since the first public whipping is enormous. Everywhere in the world Raif receives awards for his uncompromising advocacy of freedom of expression and opinion. In December 2015 the European Parliament awarded him the Sakharov Prize for Freedom of Thought, an award that Nelson Mandela won before him. The authors' association PEN honored my husband with its Pinter Prize. At the Geneva Summit for Human Rights he won the Courage Award. The German national broadcaster Deutsche Welle gave him the Freedom of Speech Award. The first Raif Badawi Award for Courageous

Journalists was bestowed at the German National Media Ball; it went to the Moroccan journalist Ali Anouzla. And what makes me particularly proud is that Raif has been nominated for the Nobel Peace Prize. These awards give him a lot of strength while he's in jail. He's told me that often. However humiliating the conditions of his imprisonment, however inhumane the physical abuse that he has to endure: these accolades show Raif that his commitment has not been in vain. That his fight for freedom of the press and freedom of opinion has been noticed by the world, and that it is bearing fruit. That knowledge alone makes martyrdom more bearable for him.

Sometimes it's just small signs. A postcard from an Amnesty group in Munich asking me to persevere. Or the barmen in Sherbrooke who have named their drinks after Raif. The legendary Irish rock band U2 devoting a concert to Raif. And the woman in the supermarket who whispers to me at the chilled food counter, "I'm on your side, Mrs. Badawi. Please say hello to your husband!"

Politicians from all over the world have also shown solidarity with Raif. Shortly after the first fifty lashes had been delivered, I was invited to Ottawa to address the Parliament. The MPs' sympathy with our fate was truly overwhelming. Afterward many Canadian politicians came to see me and promised me their support.

Exactly the same thing happened to me in Europe, where I went a few months later. Whether in Oslo, Berlin, Brussels or Paris, politicians everywhere have been on my side and Raif's. There is hardly a high-ranking visitor to Riyadh today who doesn't inquire about my husband's fate—even if it regularly causes diplomatic displeasure. One of the first

was Prince Charles, who asked about Raif in a private discussion with King Salman. The German foreign minister,
Frank-Walter Steinmeier, protested against the treatment
of my husband on a visit to the kingdom in the autumn of
2015, while the Swedish foreign minister Margot Wallström
announced: "In my opinion it is a medieval punishment."
Even American President Barack Obama has been asked by
his congressmen to take a public position on the case.

The free world has been raining rebukes and appeals
down on Riyadh. Raif has become a kind of matter of state. It
makes continuing the punishment rather awkward, because
of course Saudi Arabia doesn't want to become an international bogeyman where human rights are concerned. On the
other hand the country fears its mutinous youth — and wants
to send out a signal that it will be harsh in its treatment of
bloggers and dissidents. What the outcome of this internal
wrangling might be is impossible to predict.

Even the USA and the European Union recently appealed to
the government of the kingdom at least to release Raif from the
physical part of his punishment. But Saudi Arabia is thin-skinned
in its reaction to such appeals. It resists "interference." Raif,
according to a declaration from the Saudi Ministry of Foreign
Affairs, is a "Saudi citizen, who was accused by an independent
national and fair court, which permits no intervention in its decisions." When I read something like that I don't know whether to
laugh or cry!

Even though international attention is currently focused
on Raif, we must never forget that he stands for all the other
political prisoners in jail under the harshest conditions in Saudi
Arabia, because they have stood up in one way or another for
human rights and freedom of opinion. I've already mentioned

Walid. While Andrea and I were finalizing the book proofs in January 2016 we received bad news: Samar, Raif's sister and Walid's wife, had been arrested. She has been sent to the same prison as her brother and husband. Their fate, like that of thousands of others, is completely uncertain. Of course I wish for nothing in the world so much as that Raif will come home to us. Home to us in Canada. But in fact Raif has always been working to change something about the political system in our homeland. That's how he ended up in jail—and with him lots of other brave men and women from Saudi Arabia.

We were devastated by the news which arrived early in June 2015, that our country's supreme court had confirmed the sentence against Raif in all its barbaric harshness. That was the last authority that could have corrected the injustice through legal channels. Now only our new king himself can pardon Raif. All my hope rests on the possibility that King Salman might in the end be magnanimous enough to do so.

Here in Sherbrooke, however, we firmly expect that Raif will come and join us. When Najwa, Dodi, Miriam and I recently moved house, we asked Raif very precisely how we should decorate the new flat, and what color we should paint the walls so that he would feel at home there.

Sometimes the children and I imagine the day when we collect Raif from Montreal airport and bring him home. Dodi has confided to me that he will then—like in the movies—run toward his father in slow motion and float into his arms.

I imagine us driving in an open-topped car along the streets of Sherbrooke. Probably I myself would like to be at the wheel, because I'm taking driving lessons and will soon be taking my test. Raif will be very surprised by then. Perhaps it will be a Friday, the day when we normally hold our vigil for Raif in front of the town hall. But on that day we will hold a big buffet in front of the building—and all of my friends will meet Raif at last.

Otherwise, after such a long separation there will of course be a new wedding feast. That's obvious. I didn't particularly like the one we had in Saudi Arabia. This time I will only invite the people who have supported us. Our real family. Not the tiresome relatives who made our lives difficult in Jizan and Jeddah. And at last I will wear the golden dress that I wanted at my first wedding. It's going to be beautiful.

# ACKNOWLEDGMENTS

For their intense and valuable support on this project we would like to thank Raif's spokeswoman, Elham Manea, our agent Christine Proske of Ariadne-Buch in Munich and her New York partner Barbara Zitwer, as well as our translator Savane Al-Hassani.

*Ensaf Haidar and Andrea C. Hoffmann*